Truancy in English Secondary Schools
The Report

Contents

Acknowledgements

The research team would very much like to thank the DFE for providing the financial wherewithal to facilitate this research. We are also grateful to the LEAs and schools which took part. Participation was voluntary and these are busy places. We should like to express our gratitude to our Academic Consultants, Professors David Marsland and Brian Davies. We are especially indebted to our Statistical Consultant, Colin Coldman, who worked mightily in our aid. Our thanks are also due to Sean Gabb for sifting through the literature search and contributing Chapter Two.

We could not have managed all the fieldwork without the careful and enthusiastic support of our field researchers. We should like to express our gratitude in respect of this to Hadyn Adams, Delia Cook, Bill Dean, Dr Cecily Gale, Nigel Gann, John Grove, Alan Hartley, Dorothy Haydock, Sheila Higgins, Donald Hill, Margaret Hill, Joyce Kallevik, Dr John Mercer, Lawrence Norcross, Ben Probert, Beverley Shaw, Gerry Strode and Jennifer Wallace.

We are indebted to the DFE Steering Committee for its constant advice and encouragement. In this instance a particular debt is owed to Professor John Gray. We also received much friendly advice from Margaret Nicholls and HMI Tom Wylie and are very appreciative of the detailed notes given to us by Beryl Radford.

We are very grateful to the University of North London for its constant support for our work. We are especially pleased to thank the Internal Steering Group set up to help. Our thanks to Dr Greg Condry and Professor Mike Newman for their encouragement and interest. An especial expression of gratitude is due to Professor Alistair Ross for his unfailing enthusiasm and critical eye.

Finally an historical debt is owed to Stuart Sexton for his help and encouragement across the years. The Project Director also enjoyed the critical and searching support of Nigel Morgan, Christopher Monckton and Sir Alfred Sherman during his association with Policy Search in the middle and late 1980s. Without the help of these gentlemen the project would probably never have got underway.

University of North London truancy unit

Dr Dennis O'Keeffe   Director
Patricia Stoll   Deputy Director

Truancy Research Project, 1991–1992

Dr Dennis O'Keeffe   Director of Project
Patricia Stoll   Deputy Director Responsible for Field Research
Hilda Cole   Deputy Director Responsible for Research Methods

Consultants and Contributors:
Colin Coldman, Lowestoft College, Statistical Consultant
Sean Gabb, Author and Historian
Professor David Marsland, West London Institute of Higher Education,
        Academic Consultant
Professor Brian Davies, University of Wales, Academic Consultant

University of North London Truancy Unit
Truancy Research Project, 1991–2
Truancy in English secondary schools
a Summary

The Truancy Research Project was set up at the University of North London (formerly Polytechnic of North London) in September 1991. It was financed by the Department for Education (formerly the Department of Education and Science) with a research grant of £184,000. Its specific brief was to chart the scale and try to uncover the likely causes of truancy in English schools, in Years 10 and 11, with reference especially to Post Registration Truancy (PRT), though parallel investigation of Blanket Truancy (BT), in which children absent themselves from school without legitimate cause, was also undertaken as a condition of grant.

The survey investigated both Blanket Truancy (BT) – which is defined as unjustified absence from school of pupils who have not registered in school – and Post Registration Truancy (PRT) – which is defined as absence from lessons of pupils who have registered in school, either at the morning or afternoon registration. This latter version of truancy may be further subdivided according to whether or not the truant left the school building.

Further conditions of grant included the requirements that no child, school or Local Education Authority (LEA) would be named in the findings.

Twenty LEAs were chosen by random selection and then contacted for permission to approach their schools. None refused. Every fourth school in each LEA was then contacted, and eighty per cent agreed to participate. Those refusing were replaced by the next schools on the LEA lists.

Methodology

This was dictated both by questions of research anonymity and hoped-for consistency, and, given the scale of the project, by reasons of cost.

Confidential questionnaires were issued to all participating pupils (37,683), making the project the largest school-based study of truancy ever undertaken in this country. Resources did not permit interview or other direct back-up study of pupils; but a questionnaire was devised for completion by headteachers or delegated senior staff, with a view to providing some qualitative as well as some minimal quantitative evidence against which the findings from the pupil data could be compared. In the event, when the primary data from the pupils' questionniare responses were collated and analysed, it was apparent that a commendable consist-ency had been achieved, with only minor wastage through contradictory answers.

Results

Just under a third of all students in Years 10 and 11 (30.5 per cent) said they had truanted at least once in the last half term. This figure extrapolates to a rate of six truancies per school year. The level was markedly higher in Year 11, however, than in Year 10.[1] Thirty eight per cent of Year 11 pupils also said they had truanted last year (when they were in Year 10) and 27 per cent of present Year 10 pupils said they had truanted in Year 9.[2]

Within the category "truanting once per half term", are concealed smaller sub-categories of much more frequent truancy. For the sample as a whole 8.2 per cent of pupils say they truant at least once a week. For the pupils in Year 11 this is at 9.9 per cent – nearly a tenth. For the sample as a whole, 18.3 per cent say they truant at least once a month and for Year 11 the level is at 24.4 per cent – almost a quarter of respondents in that year.[3]

PRT is engaged in by larger numbers of pupils than BT, but by far the largest category of truants was those engaging in both. Sixty four per cent of truants engage in both, 25.2 per cent engage in PRT only and 10.3 per cent engage in BT only.[4]

The most common reason given by truants for truanting was the wish to avoid particular lessons. Two thirds of truants (67 per cent) gave this as one of their reasons for truanting. Only 49 per cent of truants gave the wish to avoid school as one of their reasons for truanting.[5] Both percentages are high, but in the case of truants giving one reason only for truanting, lessons much outweighed school. Nineteen per cent of all truants, almost a fifth, said that they truanted only to avoid lessons. The corresponding figure for truants whose only motive was to avoid school was only 5 per cent.[6]

Dissatisfaction with lessons and with school both increase in the case of more frequent offenders, but the effect is more marked in the case of lesson dissatisfaction. There was clear evidence that the greater the frequency of truancy, the more intimate its links with pupils' dissatisfaction over aspects of specific lessons. In the largest category of truants, those engaging both in BT and PRT, 80 per cent of the most frequent offenders, those truanting once a week or more, said they did this either just to avoid lessons or for this reason among others. Even among the least frequent offenders in this mixed BT/PRT category, those truanting less than once a month, 59 per cent of truants, cited desire to miss lessons as the reason, or one of the reasons, for truanting.[7]

More frequent truancy is also associated with increasing rejection of school, but this tendency is slightly less marked. In the largest category of truants, those who say they engage in both BT and PRT, 70 per cent of the most frequent offenders, those truanting at least once a week, say either that the desire to miss school is the reason for truanting or that it is one of the reasons. With lower frequency truancy however, only 32 per cent of truants in this mixed category cite avoidance of school as the reason, or one of the reasons, for truanting.[8]

Consideration of Tables Nineteen A and Nineteen lends weight to the view that PRT is more closely linked with lesson dissatisfaction at all levels than is the case with BT. It will also confirm the tendency of BT to assume an increasing lesson-focussed character at higher levels of incidence. The specific components of dissatisfaction with lessons include such complaints as the lack of enjoyment to be found in lessons, or their irrelevance or excessive difficulty, and the unlikeable personalities of some teachers.[9]

Truancy is largely social in that it is mostly engaged in with friends;[10] but there is little sign of peer-group coercion as a determinant of the activity. Truancy is based on individual decisions, according to the expressed reasons given by our respondents. They speak of other things they wish to do which probably subsumes a large social element. But they do not say anyone is making them truant.[11]

Socio-economic and institutional variation

Boys do not truant very much more than girls overall, though the gap is quite large for Year 11.[12] On the other hand single sex education seems to have some slight favourable effects on girls' propensity to truant and unfavourable effects on boys' truancy levels. County schools are slightly more liable to truancy than non-county schools. None of these effects is very large.

The socio-economic and institutional features gleaned from the heads' questionnaires correlated only slightly with truancy, but much better with attendance levels. For example, higher than average free school meals showed up infrequently in truancy level variations, but their apparent associations with variations in attendance were dramatically in evidence. The twenty five schools with most free school meals had an average truancy level of 34.4 per cent. The twenty five schools with the fewest free meals recorded an average truancy level of 28.5 per cent. This is lower, but not very much. On the other hand, the respective absence levels were 27.7 per cent and 9.9 per cent: a very big difference.[13] Many truants were presumably away on the days the survey was carried out.

There is little evidence of widespread hostility to school and its purposes. Most pupils like school, and a majority of truants do not dislike it.[14] Though truancy levels are high in the case of some of the most important subjects in the curriculum, e.g. Maths and English, and even higher in the cases of PE and French,[15] there is no evidence of widespread alienation from school. There is some good indirect evidence of a differentially distributed pattern of school ethos – strong ethos deterring, and weak ethos encouraging – the practice of truancy. On inspection this ethos seems more strongly based on deterrence and detection than on positive intellectual approval of the curriculum. The standard curriculum clearly is not regarded unfavourably, however. Fifty eight per cent of all truants want to stay on and continue their education. This suggests internalised approval of the long-term purposes of education.

Notes and references
1. See Table Three (page 33).
2. For Year 11 pupils saying they truanted in Year 10 see Table Thirty Six (page 81). For Year 10 pupils saying they truanted in Year 9 see Table Thirty Seven (page 81).
3. See Table Two (page 31).
4. See Chart A (page 35).
5. See Table Fifteen (page 50).
6. See Table Seventeen (page 52).
7. See Table Nineteen A (page 54).
8. See Table Nineteen (page 54).
9. See Table Eighteen (page 53).
10. See Table Twenty Four (page 62).
11. See Table Twenty Three (page 60).
12. See Table Five (page 36).
13. See Table Thirty Nine (page 88).
14. See Table Thirty Two (page 71).
15. See Table Twenty One (page 57).

1 About this report

The research leading to this report was financed by a grant of £184,000 in September 1991 from the then Department of Education and Science (DES), subsequently the Department for Education (DFE). The grant had effect from September 1st 1991 to August 31st 1992. After lengthy negotiations and elaborate planning by the research team, the DFE set up an official steering committee for the project, drawn from the senior civil servants at the department, the research team itself, senior personnel in local government educational welfare service, HMI, and the educational professoriat.

Twenty LEAs: A hundred and fifty schools

It was agreed in the official contract that we would survey 150 schools, drawn randomly from Local Education Authorities in England, with a view to trying to uncover the extent and causes of truancy in Years 10 and 11, above all in relation to Post Registration Truancy (henceforth PRT). The type of truancy involved when pupils fail even to register, (henceforth Blanket Truancy BT), was not to be ignored; but given that quite a lot is known about this phenomenon, whereas systematic work on PRT is virtually non-existent in this country, other than that done recently by two of the research team,[1] it was agreed in advance that the emphasis would lie heavily on PRT. It was agreed further that all resulting data would be the property of the DFE, though the Polytechnic of North London (subsequently and henceforth the University of North London), was to provide the official aegis of the research. In September 1991 the University set up its own internal advisory committee for the research, comprising mainly senior academics, but also including representation from senior administrative staff.

Truancy: a brief conceptual note

The research was undertaken in the full understanding that truancy is a complex phenomenon. Even the decision to subdivide it into two main forms – BT and PRT – and to concentrate especially on the latter, goes only a small way towards doing justice to the complexities and variety of the phenomenon. The researchers were fully aware that there are other kinds of behaviour, such as deliberate lateness, switching off in lessons or making oneself a nuisance in school, which in the broadest sense belong to the same family of attitudes and behaviour as truancy proper. We also fully recognised that truancy can vary greatly in seriousness. The occasional cutting of a lesson does not awaken the same anxiety as persistent absence from school. Nevertheless, we regard all deliberate, unjustified absence from school or lessons by pupils as the legitimate focus of our work. The only kind of illegal absence from school which is not truancy, is absence where the pupil is not the principal party to the decision, however empirically difficult to determine that question may be. It is the decision by pupils, not the seriousness of the absence, which constitutes it as truancy. Deliberately skipping one lesson may not be 'serious' but it is truancy. What counts as seriousness does not divide between BT (serious) and PRT (not serious) but between minor or occasional and persistent or sizeable patterns of either form.

The research instruments

The main one was to be a confidential pupil questionnaire to be filled in by all pupils in Years 10 and 11 present on the days that the survey was carried out. The bulk of the data, and in particular the only direct data relating to children's experience of attendance and truancy, was to be drawn from this source. This document was to be supplemented by another less confidential document to be completed by the head or some other senior teacher allocated to the task. This was to supply some background understanding of the pupil questionnaires (See Appendices A and B).

The research period

It was agreed in consultation with the DFE, that the 'research window' for our purposes should be seen as stretching from October 1991 to Eastertime 1992. The starting date was selected to allow for schools' need to settle down after the summer vacation, a consideration which ruled out the month of September. The closing date reflected the need for the field research to be finished before the Year 11 pupils became too heavily involved in their GCSE examinations. Ideally, there is a case for temporal homogenity of the research, i.e. having every school questioned on the same day. This however is a methodology of perfection which presents insuperable administrative difficulties. Even so, it is worth noting that the field research was heavily concentrated in the Spring term of 1992, especially in the month of March. More than half the schools were surveyed during this month. There might well be a case for long-term planning which converts this contingency into a deliberate policy aiming to make the research conditions more homogeneous.

The concentration of the bulk of the research into the Spring term of 1992 was inevitable, given the need to gain permission from the LEAs and the schools for the carrying out of the research. We had hoped to have managed about a third of our schools by Christmas. This goal proved impossible to fulfil, owing to experimental difficulties in the final framing of the pupil questionnaire. On advice from our DFE steering committee, we acceded to the suggestion that this questionnaire, the core instrument of our research, should be constructed on the basis of the requirement that all pupils, including non-truants, i.e. the majority of pupils, answer all questions. During the trials this policy proved completely impossible, and we were obliged to return to our original conception of the pupil question-naire permitting non-truants to pass over questions relating only to truants. (See page 8 for more detailed discussion).

The response from LEAs

Twenty LEAs were selected at random. We then wrote to them, asking for permission for us to approach headteachers within their jurisdictions. It was stressed in our opening letter to LEAs that at all stages confidentiality of results was to be maintained, and no schools or LEAs were to be named. In no sense was it intended that the exercise was to constitute a specific government check-up on deliberately selected LEAs and schools.

The reception given to our initial letters was favourable, but of an interesting variety. Such variety related in the first instance to the speed of the response. Some LEAs answered immediately, even telephoning us to make further enquiries about the scope and nature of the research, in particular asking to see, in all confidentiality, the research instruments which we proposed to employ. Others delayed their responses as late as

December 1991, the very last possible time at which a positive answer could be given if the LEA were to take part. This variation, however, at no time implied any hint of hostility or obstruction. Rather, it became apparent that there are widely heterogeneous practices in the LEA world. Thus in some cases decisions in response to research requests seem to be taken at the top, at Chief Education Officer level, in others at some lower position of authority, not always clearly specified. It was also interesting to see how different LEAs view the problem of truancy. There are very marked differences. Sometimes truancy is regarded as a matter for Educational Welfare Services. This may mean it is seen mainly as an administrative, welfare question. Sometimes truancy is regarded as within the competence of curriculum advisors, that is, as primarily an intellectual/educational question. Sometimes it is the LEA's researchers who have the principal responsibility in this matter. There seemed, in some cases, a degree of confusion as to whose area the proposed research concerned. This perhaps lay behind the apparent tardiness of some LEAs in responding to our initial letters. The letter seems in some cases to have done the rounds, waiting for someone to claim particular responsibility for its field of enquiry. In other cases it had been mislaid and a copy was requested.

We are very pleased to report the support and enthusiasm we received from the LEAs, after some initial differences in their rates of response. There were no refusals; nor were there, indeed, any suggestions of anything other than co-operation in the research. Most of the LEA personnel with whom we spoke on the telephone readily admitted the real nature of the truancy problem. Some, until the need for randomness was explained to them, even volunteered to select particular problem schools with high truancy rates. Many such personnel, it emerged in conversation, had scarcely thought of the distinct phenomenon of PRT.

The response from the schools

In every participating LEA, every fourth school was selected and its headteacher written to. The letter to schools promised them absolute confidentiality. This was necessary as much to protect the integrity of the work as to gain the cooperation of schools. The final participation rate of schools contacted was 80 per cent. A minority of schools wrote in reply to our initial letters, with a high proportion of refusals. In a majority of cases, especially in the event of acceptance, schools waited for us to telephone them for further negotiations. In cases of refusal, the next school on the list was selected. At no time were we obliged to contact more than three schools for individual school replacement purposes.

Few reasons for refusing us access were given. The two most important were pressures of work and our inability to meet requests for the results of the survey to be made known to the schools. This latter would clearly have violated both the terms of our contract with the DFE and the methodological integrity of the research. Some schools which refused mentioned time-tabling restrictions or staffing problems, for example, headteachers away on sabbaticals. There were a few flat refusals. In most cases of refusal, however, no reason was given.

The majority of schools contacted agreed to take part on the first telephone enquiry. Though it did in some instances take up to three months to gain final acceptance, in most cases arrangements were made quite quickly. There were only two cases of refusal where negotiations had broken down after a lengthy period. In these, and other cases where schools were contacted late in the programme (the second half of the Easter term 1992) and refused to take part, the team telephoned schools on a 'cold' basis, usually gaining agreement. Though there was a vast amount of administration needed, the research programme being carried out in a relatively short period for so large a number of schools, eventually we were able to reach our target of 150 schools.

It is very pleasing to be able to report the willing and courteous contributions made by the schools. Many heads recognise the existence of the truancy phenomenon, most are well aware of the PRT problem which is our special concern, and most regard truancy as a threat to the effectiveness of schools. In many instances, heads took a personal hand in the administration of the research. At the same time, there was almost everywhere an underestimation of the scale of the problem. Most heads knew there was some truancy, but thought there was less than was the case.

Trialling and the research instruments

The research team were not given their completed contract by the DFE until September 1991. Nevertheless they had long before set in motion the business of constructing suitable research instruments. It was agreed that the first of these would be a modified version of the confidential pupil questionnaire earlier used by Patricia Stoll in the fieldwork for the book on PRT written by her and Dennis O'Keeffe and published by the Education Unit of the Institute of Economic Affairs.[2] The questionnaire was itself based on one devised with the help of colleagues at the Flinders University of South Australia, during a visiting fellowship held there by Dennis O'Keeffe in 1984. The final version of the questionnaire used in the DFE sponsored research appears in Appendix A. This questionnaire was not seen by members of school staff before its actual administration during the 1991–2 research project, though naturally school staff were given a set of administering instructions.

The decision to use confidential questionnaires as the principal source of data accumulation was entailed by the scale of the research proposed. We were well aware that questionnaires, like all research instruments, bring with them distinct disadvantages as well as advantages. In particular, it is difficult to test the reliability of the data gathered in such a way. There is a danger that children may use the confidentiality of the procedure to 'show off', claiming to have engaged in more of the behaviour in question than is in fact the case. This kind of unreliability was considered, on the advice of our statistical and research consultants, to be countered by the very scale of the number of respondents involved (it was aimed at 45,000). Indeed, the opposite problem is the more intractable one, namely that some of the most persistent truants are likely themselves to be absent (playing truant) at the very time the questionnaires are administered. The result is likely to be an underestimation of the size of the problem, this underestimation itself of unknown magnitude.

There are ways around this difficulty in part, but only in part. None escapes, moreover, the problem of huge expense. Return visits, themselves expensive, run the risk that the same unjustifiable absenteeism will occur. Alternatively, questionnaires could be left in sealed envelopes, to be filled in by absentees on their return. Apart from the expense, and the possible irritation to hard pressed school administrators, such a procedure offends against the spirit of 'homogeneous questionnaire administration'. Crudely, the pupils reached in this way are not being treated identically with the others. There is, in particular, a grave danger of contamination through contact with pupils who have already filled in the questionnaire. Nor is it certain that 'problem' pupils selected in this restricted and highlighted context would react in the same way as the previously present majority to the anonymity conditions of the original questionnaire administration. Given all these difficulties, it would seem that the best procedure, within the given constraints, is to recognise that large-scale results can be gathered at acceptable cost only by the method we chose – confidential questionnaires. We are aware, by the same token, that the results of our survey are an inevitable understatement – of unknown magnitude – of the incidence of truancy.

It is entirely possible that more accurate information could be obtained from in-depth interviews. This particular approach, however, is extraordinarily expensive; and it is by no means incontrovertible that greater accuracy could be obtained in this way. If, on the other hand, schools were required to submit returns on say, PRT, much as under the new regulations they are required to return data on BT and unauthorised absence, it is far from clear exactly how the PRT data would be gathered. There would have to be standardised forms devised for subject-teachers. These might be aided by electronic surveillance. This, however, is an unknown quantity as yet, save that it is very costly. Overall, it is not at all clear that these innovations promise anything more accurate than the University of North London's Truancy Research Project has to offer from data accumulated on the basis of confidential questionnaires. What we can be certain of is that they would incur vastly greater expense.

The headteacher questionnaire

The research team also devised a new instrument, a questionnaire to be filled in by heads or other senior staff, designed expressly to be used as a qualitative control on the primary data gathered by the pupil questionnaires. This headteacher questionnaire appears in Appendix B. It is in two parts. The first was to be filled in by schools. The second allowed the option of completion by schools or of completion during an interview between heads/senior teachers and researchers. The first concentrated largely on factual material. The second involved rather more intangible matters of impression and opinion. This questionnaire, *in toto*, was sent out before the administration of the pupil questionnaire, and schools had the option of prior completion. It was confidential, but not in the tight sense of the pupil questionnaires.

The month of September 1991, was used to try out our questionnaires extensively. This was done in two schools for the pupil questionnaire (one of inner city type, the other rural) and in six schools for the (new) headteacher questionnaire. All these schools were in London or the South East of England. All, however, were such as would have fitted naturally into our research, had they been located in any of our randomly selected LEAs. The headteacher questionnaire was not intellectually altered as a result of our trials; but on the advice of participating heads and in consultation with one of our consultants, Professor David Marsland, it was drastically reduced in size, to deflect possible offence to busy school administrations. The pupil questionnaire, which on advice from our steering group had been redesigned to require ALL pupils, truants or not, to answer all questions, needed drastic revision. In particular, the requirement that all pupils answer all questions proved a major source of confusion, especially to pupils of lower ability. There was also agreement, following the trials, that the questionnaire was slightly wordy. We agreed, accordingly, to return to the more standard procedure of having non-performers (*viz* non-truants) pass on from questions to which, if required to answer, they could only say 'no'. We also resolved to rewrite the questionnaire on a somewhat slimmed down basis. These measures were also influenced by discussion with our other academic consultant, Professor Brian Davies.

Field research

The fieldwork was somewhat held up by these revisions. This was mainly a matter of the time involved in redesigning the questionnaires, as these already existed in computerised form, and then running off the final versions. We had hoped to have completed some forty schools, i.e. roughly a third of our sample, by the end of the Christmas term, but in fact we had completed only fourteen by the time schools closed for the Christmas vacation. This made the Easter term of 1992, by the end of which it was going to be necessary to have finished the fieldwork, very pressurised administratively.

In November 1991 an advertisement was placed in a national newspaper, inviting applications from people interested in conducting field research into truancy. The response was enormous, with upwards of 400 people applying to work with the project. These numbers meant that we were able to pick people of distinguished educational and research background to help us in our work. A team of potentially excellent field researchers was formed during the Autumn term, and the first training seminars were held at the University in January 1992. The purpose of these was to give the prospective researchers a thorough insight into the background and nature of the research in which we were engaged. There was extensive discussion and analysis of the truancy phenomenon, particularly with respect to our concern with PRT. Both questionnaires were explained to the researchers in detail by the Deputy Director responsible for fieldwork coordination and, we also sought to warn them of the various pitfalls and difficulties involved in research in schools. They in turn were able to warn us of some which had not occurred to us.

These researchers included some very senior ex-personnel from educational administration, some very senior retired teachers and academics, and other people experienced in commercial and/or social scientific research. It was greatly to the benefit of the project that we were able to utilize the services of such a distinguished team.

Since the survey is a nationwide one, we necessarily had to choose our fieldworkers on a nationwide basis. We had at one time considered the possibility of employing post-graduate students for this purpose. In retrospect, it seems to us that the policy of recruiting, in the main, retired senior persons had much more to recommend it, given that handling schools with delicacy and tact is a crucial feature of the research. The nationwide character of the work also led us to seek people from specific regions of the country. This was a matter of logistics. It is not normally possible to ask fieldworkers to cover an area of much more than 100 miles in diameter. In practice we found that our expectation that one school would occupy a researcher one half day was borne out by experience. On the other hand, our hope that with LEA help we would often be able to do two schools in one LEA on the same say, proved illusory. LEAs are not able to offer that kind of coordination, and the overwhelming majority of schools preferred a morning appointment. So time, distance and cost all made it necessary to locate researchers relatively close to the schools we were asking them to investigate.

The work of our field Researchers

A system evolved by which the research team based at the University of North London would negotiate with a school regarding a day and time for the survey. A researcher in the area would then be contacted by telephone. If he/she agreed to undertake the work, full details would be sent by letter. A week before the survey was due to be carried out, the school would receive the headteacher questionnaire, instructions for administerng the pupil questionnaire and confirmation of the arrangements, including the name of the visiting researcher. In many cases this fieldwork was carried out by the three members of the research team, not only for reasons of economy, but because the team wanted to be involved as much as possible in the administering of the questionnaires.

In the event, and thanks to the efforts of our field researchers, all the work was completed in good order. As we shall see in our discussion of our results, there seems to have been commendable regularity in the way the questionnaires were administered.

References
1. Stoll, P. and O'Keeffe, D. J. *Officially Present: An Investigation into Post Registration Truancy in Nine Maintained Schools* Institute of Economic Affairs Education Unit, 1989
2. *Ibid.*

2 Truancy: its measurement and causation
A brief review of the literature
by Sean Gabb

Introduction

In this chapter are discussed some of the traditional answers given to the question – Why do children play truant? This may be regarded as an important question for a number of reasons.

First, truancy is disobedience. Children are required by law to be educated and for most people this means going to school. It is effectively the law that they go there. If they choose not to go, they are disobeying adult authority, either of their parents or of the State. If their truancy is parent-condoned, the situation is doubly unacceptable.

Second, it is said to lead to other, more tangible forms of delinquency (Tyerman, 1968). Despite some evidence to the contrary, there is a common association of truancy with crimes such as theft, criminal damage, robbery with violence, and abusive conduct. In those inner city areas where truancy patrols have been established, the incidence of these crimes has been observed to fall (Reid 1987[1]). These facts, if true, may reinforce the pessimistic view of children, which holds that they will, unless confined in school, do something by themselves, and that this will be more often bad than good. They tend also, however, to reinforce the meliorist view of children, on which rests much of the argument for a compulsory education at least subsidised and inspected by the State.

According to this view, it is possible to take a child and, away from all family influences and with peer pressures minimised so far as possible, to impart the bases of whatever is currently held to constitute good citizenship. This was the rationale behind the educational efforts of the absolutist states of old Europe. In a more liberal form, the view was advanced by the advocates of State support for education in nineteenth century England.[2] It has also been advanced, if turned on its head, by those neo-Marxists who claim that, while there undoubtedly is one, the effect on society of schooling is largely malign, in so far as it reproduces an unjust set of power relationships (Bowles and Gintis, 1976; Ramsay 1983).

Granting that school is good, the reciprocal is never far behind, that lack of schooling is bad. Thus the emphasis on the bad things children will do out of school. The idea is deeply ingrained that unschooled people must be socially incompetent, lacking in knowledge and skills and lead unenjoyable lives. Thus also, the conclusion drawn by many from the findings of a recent report correlating truancy from school with unemployment in later life.[3]

It may even be that truancy, once established in a family, becomes hereditary. Robins *et al* (1979) reported that persistent truants tend to marry each other and to encourage or tolerate truancy in their children.

Third, it may be that the meliorists are wrong, in that the relationship between truancy and the various forms of delinquency may be one of common effect rather than of cause and effect (Farrington, 1986). Perhaps there are some people disposed as children to break windows and as adults to go on the dole, who are also disposed to stay away from school. But his hypothesis, if correct, tends not to deny the usefulness of seeking an answer to our question, but instead to give new grounds for seeking one.

Fourth, there are considerations of cost. The Department for Education is responsible for 27,000 primary and secondary schools throughout England. It supplies the lion's share of finance for teachers' salaries, and provides much other educational finance. Its current spending is based on the assumption that there will be nine million children in the schools to be educated. Once committed, this money must be spent regardless of how many children are actually attending the schools. The larger the number of children absenting themselves from these schools, therefore, the greater the waste of public resources.

These are some of the reasons truancy is a subject thought worth investigating, and has been so thought – if in differing degree – for much of this century.

The meaning of truancy

An obvious preliminary question is – What exactly is truancy? None of the various Education Acts defines truancy; nor is this lack supplied in the case law. Nor, indeed, have the various researchers agreed a definition. Must every child who is absent from school, for whatever reason, be classified as a truant? This is the opinion of Reynolds and Murgatroyd (1977–cited, Galloway (1985)). The DFE category, 'authorised' absence, suggests a narrower classification. We can narrow the definition by saying that a child plays truant who is absent from school without the school's authority, so excluding those children who are certified or accepted as too ill to attend. But this still includes those children who are absent with leave given by their parents, or who are actually kept at home by their parents. For evidence that this is a reasonably common occurrence, see Galloway *et al* (1982).

Also, it may be asked if we do right always to exclude absences due to self-inflicted medical conditions or negligence. Boyson (1974) mentions the 1,200 under age girls who became pregnant in 1970.

We can narrow the definition of the truant again by following Tyerman (1968), who reserves the term for children who are absent from school purely on their own initiative. This is the definition adopted by Galloway (1985). However, Hersov (1977) goes still further, dividing from truants "school phobics" and school refusers, many of whom – depending on how they are in turn defined – will be absent on their own initiative.

Since the term has been given different meanings by different writers, the literature cannot be regarded as dealing with an homogeneous subject. Conclusions reached in one study of truants cannot automatically be regarded as supported or disputed by conclusions reached in another: care must first be taken to ensure that the same, or at least a similar, definition has been given to truancy.

The causes of truancy

According to Adams (1978):

> When it comes to analysing root causes [of truancy] there are the wildest divergencies of viewpoints and theories – the effects of a sick society, the abandonment of religious beliefs and moral values, the consequences of an unjust social and economic system, or even, as I

have heard it convincingly argued, as a result of damage done to the nervous system by excess lead in the urban atmosphere in which many of us are condemned to live and work.

But this divergence is more apparent than real. Explanations fall under two headings. Children play truant either because their schools are not so well organised in some respects as they might be, or because the children themselves are ill-equipped, typically by reason of their home backgrounds, to deal with the normal pressures of schooling. Each of these in turn will be examined.

The causes of truancy: children and their backgrounds?
In their introduction to one of the recent main texts on the subject, Hersov and Berg (1980) state with untroubled confidence that:

> The epidemiological contributions to this book clearly demonstrate the importance of age, sex, and social background in determining the prevalence of unjustifiable absence from school.

They add (see also Cooper, 1966):

> It is still uncertain to what extent factors within the school contribute to the problem . . .

This is and has been the broad consensus of opinion among researchers. There is a large body of literature, going back at least into the last century, seeking to explain truancy in terms of failings among children and their families (e.g., Kline, 1898; Healy, 1915). In the 1920s, Burt (Tyerman, 1968) elaborated the first concept of 'school phobia', describing how some children stayed away from schools that had been used by them and their parents as air raid shelters during the Great War. They associated school with fear of death and became 'neurotic' when compelled to go there. In the 1930s, there were the psychoanalytic theories of Broadwin (Tyerman, 1968), relating truancy to various complexes.

These earlier theories were not long accepted, if at all. Broadwin can be criticised for having reasoned from premises that were by no means certain, to conclusions that he made little attempt to verify by empirical research. Burt's earliest concept of school phobia could not have lasted beyond the middle 1920s, and may have been an attempt less to explain truancy than to attract larger government funding for its treatment through the use of fashionable semi-medical terms. Even so, the tradition was set. Since then, many researchers have devoted themselves to discovering what is wrong with the personalities or backgrounds, or both, of those children who play truant.

According to various primary and secondary teachers interviewed by Farrington (1980), truants were:

lazy, lacked concentration, were restless, were difficult to discipline, did not care about being a credit to their parents, and were not clean and tidy on their arrival at school.

Translated into more neutral terms, this description is seconded by much other research. The association of truancy with delinquency has been mentioned above. Otherwise, truants are said to do badly in intelligence tests (Farrington, 1980), to have low levels of self-esteem (Reid, 1982), and to tend towards unshapeliness and uncleanliness (Tyerman, 1968).

Their backgrounds are believed to be equally unfortunate. They are said to come predominantly from poor families, where the father – if actually present and working – has a job with low earnings and low status and low security (Tyerman, 1968; Farrington, 1980; Reid, 1986). They live usually in the inner cities, in bad and overcrowded properties (Tyerman, 1968, Galloway, 1985). There is a tendency for their parents not to care about punctuality or attendance or homework (Reid, 1986).

Whether – as did the teachers interviewed by Farrington (1980) – we regard truants in a moralistic light, or as the pitiable victims of circumstance, the conclusions reached by this line of research are straightforward. If children play truant, it is because they are for various reasons unable to cope with school. Truancy is their problem; and any attempt to stop them from playing truant must be concerned with readjusting them, either in terms of the deficits formed in the home or of the inadequacies in the school environment itself.

The causes of truancy: schools? (1)
However, this whole line of research has been challenged. Carroll *et al* (1977), looking at schools in South Wales, doubt if children or their

backgrounds can be the sole or even the principal cause of truancy. Reynolds and Murgatroyd (1977) are careful to show that the schools served:

> a relatively homogenous community with very small differences in the social class composition of the people who live in the catchment areas of the different schools.

Yet the study finds that patterns of deviancy and attendance vary greatly between different schools within this homogeneous catchment area. The suggestion is that the schools themselves play at least some part in causing these variable rates. Rutter *et al* (1979), investigating twelve Inner London schools, reach much the same conclusion.

This research has been questioned. Galloway (1985) draws attention to the small numbers of pupils examined in the Carroll *et al* study – ranging between seventeen and sixty. His main objection is that there may have been a significant heterogeneity in the social backgrounds of the children despite the care taken to show their homogeneity. He concedes that there may be some truth in the results – as do Reynolds *et al* (1980) – but stresses what he believes are the:

> methodological difficulties in demonstrating the differences between schools [which] are due to factors within the schools and not to factors in their catchment areas.

Another reason why such research is often questioned – indeed, why it forms so small a part of the total of the research into truancy (Galloway, 1985) – is that it disturbs many of the researchers' most basic assumptions. It has been suggested that, irrespective of how good the evidence may be, the choice of where mainly to seek evidence has been prompted by considerations other than pure academic curiosity.

There is the persistent belief, mentioned above, that schooling is good. Reynolds *et al* (1980) – (see also Jones, 1980) – note how hard it is, on ideological grounds, for many educational researchers to accept that, at times, it may not be good. This reluctance may sometimes have been increased by professional self-interest. Reynolds *et al* (1980), for example, describe how what might have been an interesting survey of how schools generate delinquency, was frustrated in 1971 by the Inner London Educational Authority and the National Union of Teachers working together: non-cooperation, coupled with threats of industrial action, ensured that the research was cut short.

Yet there is a body of theoretical and empirical literature which looks to school itself as a cause of truancy. As we have seen, Carroll (1977) doubts if deficiencies in children or their backgrounds can be the sole or even the principal cause of truancy. He finds that patterns of deviancy and attendance vary greatly between different schools within the same, homogeneous catchment area. Such differences in these rates, he suggests, cannot be wholly related to the children.

Cloward and Ohlin (1961) regard truancy as part of a wider delinquency caused by 'blocked opportunity' within school. Working class children begin their school careers reasonably confident about their aims and ambitions in life. But the middle class bias of school tends to denigrate these aims and ambitions and to put others in their place that the children dislike, but lack the sophistication consciously to examine and reject. The result is a disaffection with school and its ideals that can result in delinquency.

Mays (1964), writing of working class children in Liverpool, comments that delinquency is:

> not so much a symptom of maladjustment as of adjustment to a sub-culture, in conflict with the culture of the city as a whole.

Cicourel and Kituse (1963) look more to the structure of relationships within school between teachers and pupils, how these progressively erode the self-esteem of working class pupils and produce feelings of inferiority that, again, lead to delinquent behaviour.

Such broadly is the view taken by Carlen, Gleeson and Wardhaugh (1992). They accept the traditional description of truants as children with what are normally defined as 'problems', but go on to claim that the whole present structure of society, and not only schools, is responsible for truancy. There is, they say, 'much pain, hurt and suffering around current educational arrangements' that derive from the pre-occupations of the last century with social control and the 'normalisation' of the new working class. The marginalisation of certain categories of children by the present system of schooling forces them into truancy as a 'mode of resistance'. This in turn gives the authorities an excuse to control 'families living at the margins of respectability', so reinforcing their 'social exclusion'.

Less ambitious than Carlen, Gleeson and Ward, other neo-Marxists have looked into the effect of the curriculum alone on truancy. Ramsay (1983) refers to the:

claim that knowledge is being used as a form of social control.

Behind the facade of Maths and English, he repeats, there is said to be a 'hidden curriculum' to keep working class and ethnic minority children in their places. Truancy is, in part, a protest against this pressure.

Some negative evidence in support of these views can be seen in the better attendance figures supposedly enjoyed by some schools that adopt a non-racist, non-classist curriculum (Ramsay 1983).

A similar importance has been claimed for the effect of the curriculum on truancy from an opposite political position. Thus Boyson (1974):

The increase in truancy has gone hand in hand with the schools' retreat from their primary task of schooling. Pupils know that the emphasis on 'liberation', 'social orientation' and 'life-enhancement' has little relevance to them and is simply a means whereby their teachers act out their own frustrations . . . Ordinary boys and their parents know that schools are for schooling and they see little point in attending schools which cease to offer it.

This brings us to another curriculum-based explanation of truancy. Before moving further, however, it is necessary, to pause and look again at the concept of truancy – not this time at its meaning so much as at its measurement.

The measurement of truancy
One of the most basic questions facing any truancy researcher is – How many children fail to attend school? Once a figure has been found, it can be fitted into the various conceptual schemes to see what proportion of

absences can and cannot be ascribed to truancy. But the figure must be found in the first place. The great majority of researchers find this by looking in the morning and afternoon registers of attendance kept by the schools and passed on to the local education authorities. This is where Tyerman (1968), for example, finds the data with which he supports his view that:

annual rate of absence from school is about 10 per cent.

And that:

more than half the children who regularly play truant are malajusted, and their truancy is a warning that they may be developing delinquent tendencies.

For all their differences over definition, the common reliance on the attendance registers allows most researchers to settle on a truancy rate of around 15 per cent.

The problem is, however, that the registers may not reflect attendance accurately. Cameron (1974), commenting on an Inner London Education Authority truancy survey – showing an average secondary school attendance rate in 1974 of 84.6 per cent (ILEA, 1975) – claimed that the registers were 'wide-open to rigging' by head teachers and other interested persons. More important though than casual fraud, is the possibility that the attendance registers are systematically under-reporting the scale of non-attendance.

According to Williams (1974):

The most serious deficiency of the register is that it misses completely the children who skip class after the count is taken at the beginning of the morning and afternoon sessions.

He follows this with several passages of anecdotal evidence, indicating the potentially large scale of the problem – and therefore its refuting effect on much of the standard categorising of truants – but makes no effort to analyse or refine his own term 'post registration truancy'. Following this introduction of the subject, Galloway (1976) looks briefly at 'hidden truancy', and Reid (1985) at 'specific lesson absence'. But it is O'Keeffe (1981) who first uses the term Post Registration Truancy in a sytematic way, and develops from it an alternative curriculum-based theory of truancy.

The causes of truancy: school? (2)

Reynolds (1976) was the first author to consider the possibility that the causes of truancy may lie significantly within the world of school itself. Working on male truancy in secondary modern schools in Wales he showed that truancy seems strongly influenced by school organisation.

On the other hand, most literature until recently did not divide truancy into sub-types. In his first study of the subject, O'Keeffe (1981) divides truancy into two types. There is 'Blanket' Truancy, where the child stays completely away from school, and which has been the only object of much study. Then there is Post Registration Truancy, where 'the child is marked officially present at school, but is subsequently absent from some/all lessons'. He claims that, while no systematic research had yet been done here, 'such truancy is on a huge scale'.

Moreover, according to Stoll and O'Keeffe (1989), the scale of Post Registration Truancy escalated throughout the 1980s. They cite a spot check on attendance among 4th year pupils in a North London comprehensive school. The average attendance during a particular lesson was found to be 64 per cent. A year later, the spot check was repeated on the same pupils. Their average attendance had declined to 61 per cent.

Starting in 1985, Stoll and O'Keeffe headed a three year research project to identify the scale and causes of both Blanket and Post Registration Truancy. They studied 105 pupils as they moved through their third, fourth and fifth years at a mixed comprehensive school in North London. Data was collected from the pupils directly via questionnaires, anonymity was assured but stringent controls were imposed on the analysis of the data, to mimise untruthfulness.

This was a novel approach, in so far as earlier researchers – e.g., Tyerman (1968) – had confined their attention to those truanting children referred to them by educational psychologists. Since only a small minority of children are ever sent to a psychologist, it is possible that all the research concerning their truancy is correct – but that they form only a small minority of truants; and few conclusions, if any, derived from observing them can be applied to truants in general. By setting their pupil question-naires, Stoll and O'Keeffe were seeking to discover first the true scale of truancy, and then, this established, its commonest causes.

The initial results showed a 'staggeringly high number of truants' (Stoll and O'Keeffe, 1989). 66 per cent of pupils confessed to having truanted at some time during their secondary schooling – 50 per cent Post Registration, 5 per cent Blanket, and 11 per cent combined. 57 per cent of the 66 per cent confessed to truanting at least once a month; and 72 per cent of the 57 per cent confessed to doing so still more frequently. These rates increased during the fourth and fifth years.

The great majority of truants claimed to dislike specific lessons – e.g. Science, French and Games – rather than school as a whole. 54 per cent of third years replying said that they liked school, most of the remainder at least believing that they were learning something useful.

With Stoll and O'Keeffe directing, a Truancy Research Unit was set up in 1989 to look at truancy throughout the country. The same methods were used, and much the same results were reached. Truancy was widespread, mostly Post Registration. High among stated reasons was the obligation to complete a lot of course work for the GCSE examinations – mostly for English and Mathematics.

Without giving much critical attention to the earlier literature – other than to note its methodological limitations – Stoll and O'Keeffe claim that Post Registration Truancy is the most common type, and that its causes are 'principally a curricular issue'.

This remains a minority position. So does their stress on Blanket Truancy and Post Registration Truancy as separate categories. Work published in the early 1980s by Gray, McPherson and Raffe admitted that it is more plausible to locate the cases of truancy in school rather than in the home. These authors admitted, too, the likely rational character of the act of truancy. Recent work by Gray and Jesson (1990), however, has not taken these insights further. They draw on the Youth Cohort Study of England and Wales, which is a national survey of young people's experiences of school, work, post-compulsory education and training (see Gray *et al* 1989). They draw attention to a question asked of and answered by more than 40,000 young people:

Did you play truant in your fifth year at School?

The size of the sample is impressive. The drawback is that the members of the sample were questioned only after they had left school. There is thus a lack of contemporaneity about the results. Their school experiences overlaid by other impressions, it may be that many of the young people questioned about whether they truanted and if so how often, were giving answers at variance with what actually happened. They are being asked to give answers to questions with all the benefit of hindsight. The Stoll and O'Keeffe research concentrates on young people still at school, asking about their present experience.

Second, though familiar with O'Keeffe's work, Gray and Jesson make no sharp distinction between Blanket and Post Registration Truancy. They prefer instead to distinguish truancy only on the basis of hours spent away from school – between 'serious' and 'selective' truancy. Thus the possible answers to their question are:

For weeks at a time
For several days at a time
For particular days or lessons
For the odd day or lesson
Never.

Though mention is made of 'lessons', there is no plain and explicit question about consistent Post Registration Truancy. This is a serious gap. By their own use of questionnaires, however, they have tacitly admitted the Stoll and O'Keeffe claims about the methodological limitations of the earlier research tradition.

Nevertheless, though suggestive and so far unrefuted, the Stoll and O'Keeffe research has still to replace conclusively its earlier rivals. It remains to be seen whether, and if so how far, this new research invalidates the still vigorous mainstream view of truancy as a reflection of deficiencies in the children or their backgrounds, or if the two can be combined to form a new and fruitful synthesis.

Bibliography

Adams, F. *The Benefits of an Interdisciplinary Approach to the Question of Disruptive Pupils* Education, 3rd February, 1978, p. 91.

Bowles, S. and Gintis, H. *Schooling in Capitalist America* Routledge and Kegan Paul, London, 1976.

Boyson, R. *The Need for Realism* in Turner, 1974.

Burt, C. *The Young Delinquent* London University Press, London, 1925.

Cameron, S. *Truancy Survey Wide Open to Rigging By Heads* Times Educational Supplement, 2nd August, 1974.

Carlen, P., Gleeson, D. and Wardhaugh, J. *Truancy: The Politics of Compulsory Schooling* Open University Press, Buckingham, 1992.

Carroll, H. C. M. (ed.) *Absenteeism in South Wales: Studies of Pupils, their Homes and their Secondary Schools* University College, Swansea, 1977.

Cicourel, A. V. and Kituse, J. I. *The Educational Decision Makers* Bubbs Merrill, New York, 1963.

Cloward, R. A. and Ohlin, R. E. *Delinquents and Opportunity* Routledge and Kegan Paul, London, 1961.

Cooper, M. G. *School Refusal: An Inquiry into the Part Played by Schools* Educational Research, 8, 1966.

Farrington, D. *Truancy, Delinquency, the Home and School* in Hersov and Berg, 1980.

Fitzherbert, K. *Unwillingly to School* New Society, 17th February 1977.

Galloway, D. *Size of School, Socio-Economic Hardship, Suspension Rates and Persistent Unjustified Absence from School* British Journal of Educational Psychology, 46, 1976.

Galloway, D. *Schools and Persistent Absentees* Pergamon Press, 1985.

Galloway, D., Ball, T., Blomfield, D. and Seyd, R. *Schools and Disruptive Children* Longman, Harlow, 1982.

Gray, J., McPherson, A. F. and Raffe, D. *Reconstructions of Secondary Education* RKP, 1983.

Gray, J., Jesson, D., Pattie, C. and Sime, N. *Education and Training Opportunities in the Inner City* Training Agency Research and Development Series, no. 51, Sheffield, 1989.

Gray, J., Jesson, D. *Truancy in Secondary Schools amongst Fifth Year Pupils* (revised version January 1990), QQSE Research Group Educational Research Centre, Sheffield University.

Healy, W. *The Individual Delinquent* Heinemann, London, 1915.

Hersov, L. *School Refusal* in Rutter, M. and Hersov, L. *Child Psychiatry: Modern Approaches* Oxford, Oxford University Press, 1977.

Hersov, L. and Berg, I. (eds.) *Out of School* John Wiley, Chichester, 1980.

ILEA (Inner London Educational Authority) *Non-Attendance and Truancy* Report of the Schools Sub-Committee to the Educational Committee, 1975.

Jackson, M. *The Short Step from Truancy to the Dole Queue*, Times Educational Supplement, 17th October, 1986.

Jones, A. *The School's View of Persistent Absenteeism*, in Hersov and Berg, 1980.

Kline, L. W. *The Migratory Impulse versus the Love of home*, American journal of Psychology, 10, 1898.

Macaulay, T. B., speech in the House of Commons, 18th April, 1847, in The Miscellaneous Writings and Speeches of Lord Macaulay, Longmans, Green and Co., London, 1889.

May, D. *Truancy, School Absenteeism and Delinquency* Scottish Educational Studies, 7, 1975.

Mays, J. B. *Growing up in the City* Liverpool University Press, Liverpool, 1964.

Mill, J. S. *On Liberty* (1859), Chapter V, Applications, 'Everyman' edition, J. M. Dent & Sons Ltd, London, 1972.

O'Keeffe, D. J. *Labour in Vain: Industry, Truancy and the School Curriculum* in Flew, A. (ed.) *The Pied Pipers of Education* Social Affairs Unit, London, 1981.

O'Keeffe, D. J. (ed.) *The Wayward Curriculum* Social Affairs Unit, London, 1986.

Ramsay, P. *Fresh Perspectives on the School Transformation – Reproduction Debate: A Response to Anyon from the Antipodes* Curriculum Enquiry, 13, 1983.

Reid, K. *The Self-Concept and Persistent School Absenteeism* British Journal of Educational Psychology, 1982.

Reid, K. *Truancy and School Absenteeism* Hodder and Stoughton, London, 1985.

Reid, K. *Truancy and School Absenteeism: The State of the Art, Maladjustment and Therapeutic Education* Volume 4, part 3, 1986.

Reid, K. and Kendall, L. *A Review of Some Recent Research in Persistent School Absenteeism* British Journal of Educational Studies, Volume 30, part 3, October 1982.

Reid, K. (ed.) *Combating School Absenteeism* Hodder and Stoughton, London, 1987.

Reynolds, D., *The Delinquent School* in Hammersley, M. and Wood, P. *The Process of Schooling* Routledge and Kegan Paul, 1976.

Reynolds, D. and Murgatroyd, S. *The Sociology of Schooling and the Absent Pupil: The School as a Factor in the Generation of Truancy* in Carroll, 1977.

Reynolds, D., Jones, D., St. Leger, S. and Murgatroyd, S. *School Factors and Truancy* in Hersov and Berg, 1980.

Robins, L. A., Ratcliffe, K. S. and West, P. A. *School Achievement in Two Generations: A Study of 88 Black urban Families* in Shamsie, S. J. (ed.) *New Directions in Childrens' Mental Health* Spectrum, New York, 1979.

Rutter, M., Maughan, B., Mortimore, P., Ouston, J. and Smith, A. *Fifteen Thousand Hours: Secondary Schools and their Effects on Pupils* Open Books, London, 1979.

Stoll, P. A. *Post Registration Truancy: A Study* Thesis submitted to the Polytechnic of North London, June 1989.

Stoll, P. A. and O'Keeffe, D. J. *Officially Present: An Investigation into Post-Registration Truancy in Nine Maintained Secondary Schools* Institute of Economic Affairs, London, 1989.

Turner, B. (ed.) *Truancy* Ward Lock Educational, London, 1974.

Tyerman, M. (ed.) *Truancy* University of London Press, London, 1968.

(Webb, S., signed article, The Guardian, 18th October, 1983).

Williams, P. *Collecting the Figures* in Turner, 1974.

Notes

1. See also *multa inter alia*: Reid and Kendall (1982) – noting that the association had been established for more than 50 years; Fitzherbert (1977) – describing truancy as a training in deviancy; Tyerman (1968) –

   'If a boy finds that he can successfully avoid going to school, it is a step to believing that he can just as easily succeed with other offences'; and Burt (1925) – seeking regular verification for an hypothesis already believed to be true.

   It is not true, however, that truancy and delinquency can be perfectly associated. As will be seen later, not all truants may be or will become delinquents. Nor may even a large minority of delinquent children also be truants. According to Webb (1983), 'the Met's juvenile crime statistics for Inner London . . . show that less than 4 per cent of offenders were truanting at the time of their crime'.

2. See, for example, Macaulay (1889):

   'It is the duty of Government to protect our persons and property from danger. The gross ignorance of the common people is a principal cause of danger to our persons and property. Therefore, it is the duty of the Government to take care that the common people shall not be grossly ignorant.'

   See also Mill (1972):

   'It still remains unrecognised, that to bring a child into existence without a fair prospect of being able, not only to provide food for its body but instruction and training for its mind, is a moral crime, both against the unfortunate offspring and against society; and that if the parent does not fulfill this obligation, the State ought to see it fulfilled, at the charge, so far as possible, of the parent.'

3. See Mark Jackson (1986), reporting on the Youth Cohort Study:

   'About half the youngsters in the report admitted having played truant. But while two thirds had only skipped the odd day or lesson, the 15 per cent of those who were unemployed a year after leaving school had been the most regular truants, and almost one in five of them said they had stayed away for days or weeks at a time.'

See also Farrington (1986):

'It seems that, after leaving school, the truants tend to develop a markedly antisocial or deviant life style.'

3 The size of the problem

Introduction

The survey investigated both Blanket Truancy (BT) – which is defined as unjustified absence from school of pupils who have not registered in school – and Post Registration Truancy (PRT) – which is defined as absence from lessons of pupils who have registered in school, either at the morning or afternoon registration. This latter version of truancy may be further subdivided according to whether or not the truant left the school building. The survey team is keenly aware, as was noted in the first chapter, that there are other forms of behaviour somewhat akin to truancy, such as deliberate lateness for school or lessons, disruptive behaviour in class or persistent failure to pay attention in class. Although such behaviour may be thought of as constituting 'near-truancy', the research was not investigating these phenomena and the questionnaires contained no questions designed to elicit direct information regarding them.

Considerably more pupils (45,414) should have completed questionnaires than did so (37,683). Thus overall there were 7,731 non-respondents on the days when the questionnaires were administered in their schools – some 17 per cent. It is impossible to say how many of these absentees were engaging in BT or PRT. Quite clearly, many pupils must have been away for legitimate reasons – illness or work experience, for example. One assumes, nevertheless, minimally, that the numbers of truants would be at least up to the sample average of about a third of all respondents admitting to some kind of truancy in the last half term. (See below). Even with this deficit of more than seven thousand non-respondents, however, the figure in the second bracket above represents the largest school-based study of truancy ever mounted in this country.

Overall numbers of pupils and their response rate are shown in Table One.

Table One
Overall number of pupils and their response rates

Year 10	Total pupils	22,521
	Total questionnaires	19,305
	Response rate	82.7%
Year 11	Total pupils	22,893
	Total questionnaires	18,253
	Response rate	79.7%
All pupils	Total pupils	45,414
	Total questionnaires	37,683
	Response rate	83.0%

NB The total number of questionnaires shown in Table One is larger than the sum of Year 10 and 11 pupils, owing to some pupils' having failed to state their Year on the questionnaires. There was also a small actual loss of data through inconsistent filling in of questionnaires.[1]

Some absentees will be truants. The difficulty, we repeat, is that there is no sure way of ascertaining what proportion of them are. This is a problem we shall deal with more fully later. Suffice it here to note the undeniable underestimation built into the research by the absence from school or lessons of an unknown number of truants on the days when the pupil questionnaires were administered. Nor do returns merely underestimate the *numbers* of pupils admitting to having engaged in any kind of truancy, even as little as once in the last half term. They are also an underestimation of the *frequency* of truancy. The pupils who were absent are also likely to be more frequent in their truancy.[2]

Thus we have felt constrained to accept that while the figures we do have are already consistent with significant levels of truancy, both in the form of BT and PRT, our results systematically understate the problem. It is proper, then, to stress that the situation is worse than the results show.

Two measures of truancy level are used. Where the result is best given in terms of overall percentages, the sample is taken to be all the respondents. Where comparisons are made between schools, the sample is taken to be the 150 schools surveyed, and the mean truancy level is the mean of the levels of truancy in the 150 individual schools. The differences between these measures is small. For example, overall, 30.5 per cent of all pupils truanted at some time while the mean truancy level for all schools is 31 per cent.

The scale and frequency of truancy

The overall scale and frequency of truancy (truancy understood here to embrace any type of truancy) are shown in Table Two.

Table Two
Levels and frequency of truancy (any type)

Base: all pupils

	All	Year 10	Year 11
Every day	1.5	1.3	1.6
2–4 times a week	3.2	2.6	3.8
Once a week	3.5	2.5	4.5
2–3 times a month	5.4	4.0	6.8
Once a month	4.7	4.0	5.5
Less often	12.2	10.8	13.6
Never	69.5	74.8	64.2

It should be stressed that this table relates to all *pupils* and not all truants. It needs to be stressed also that the time categories are discrete. Thus in the 'All' column, 1.5 per cent of all pupils are truanting every day, a further 3.2 per cent are doing so 2–4 times a week, and so on. Each column can be summed up to and including the last time category of less often than once a month. The sum of pupils in the 'All' column admitting to truancy of any kind in the last half term is 30.5 per cent of all pupils. It should be emphasised again that this figure subsumes a number of smaller levels of higher frequency truancy, as revealed in the table. It is not a vacuous shell concealing insignificant inner levels.

It is noteworthy, for example, that overall 8.2 per cent of pupils are truanting once a week or more and that in Year 11 this rises to 9.9 per cent, or almost one in ten of all Year 11 pupils. If we look at pupils who truant at least once a month, we find for the sample as a whole, a figure of 18.3 per cent. If we look at the same statistic for Year 11 only, we have a figure of 22.2 per cent. More than one in five of Year 11 pupils, on these figures, say they are truanting at least once a month.

The figues are understatements of the problem

It is true in Table Two the 'Never' category remains the largest by far, though it falls considerably between Years 10 and 11, from almost three quarters of pupils to something below two thirds. But for those pupils who do truant, the figures are, nevertheless, understatements. First, in the case of pupils who truant often, there is the absence of many pupils who would have been asked about truanting if they had been present. In the case of every day truants or those who say they play truant 2–4 times a week, this inevitably means quite a large number. The survey systematically understates the truancy problem.

In this instance, moreover, there is another source of understatement. The children were asked if they had ever engaged in BT or PRT, the latter involving either leaving or not leaving the building. In constructing our presentation of their answers, we have in the case of all pupils saying they have truanted, shown only the largest category, or chosen indifferently if the categories are equal. For example, in the case of pupils who say the have engaged in BT and either or both the two forms of PRT once a week, they have been counted as truanting only once a week. Thus, what already seems sizeable levels of truancy according to the pupils' responses to the questionnaires, e.g. nearly 10 per cent of pupils in Year 11 saying they truant at least once a week, contain considerable understatements of the extent of the phenomenon.

There is therefore a real problem, not just a minor problem of large numbers of pupils truanting occasionally. This background consideration has to be borne in mind as we make our way through the detailed results.

Pupils truanting in Years 10 and 11

We may safely assume that educational arrangements will never achieve 100 per cent attendance; nor does the opposite extreme of 100 per cent truancy seem remotely likely. Our findings undoubtedly show, however, that there is a great deal of truancy in schools, both in the form of BT and of PRT. There is also a marked difference between schools. We may conveniently in the first instance approach the findings by way of overall percentages of truanting pupils, engaging in BT, PRT or both. The figures are compiled on the basis of all pupils who admitted any kind of truancy at all in the last half term, though we have separated the types. As we have seen, the figures for overall truancy are a few percentage points higher than those specifically relating to PRT. In fact 30.5 per cent (a bit less than a third) of all pupils in the survey admitted to truanting in the half term prior to the day of the survey.

It should be stressed that truancy levels are high both for Year 10 and Year 11, and especially Year 11, as is revealed in Table Three. The aggregate figures are based on pupils admitting to any kind of truancy within the last half term. Many respondents will have committed no more than the seemingly minor infraction of one act of truancy. But it should be noted that such an admission of a single occasion of truancy would, if sustained, add up to a rate of six times per school year.

There is some preliminary evidence that this extrapolation itself underestimates annual truancy levels. These levels come out higher when pupils are asked to say whether they have truanted across a whole year rather than merely across the half term of our survey. (See Table Thirty Six, page 81; and Table Thirty Seven, page 81). We repeat, there are concealed within the global figures smaller groups of more persistent truancy. The global figures are presented now; more detailed discussion follows later in the text.

Table Three presents the data for BT only, PRT only and both in combination, for the whole sample and also divided into Years 10 and 11. PRT is not here broken down into leaving or not leaving the building.

Table Three
Truancy levels in Years 10 and 11

Base: all pupils

	Year 10	Year 11	All pupils
	%	%	%
BT only	3	3	3
PRT only	6	9	7
BT & PRT	16	24	20
All truants	25	36	31

It is important to note again one of the central results of the survey: truancy levels rise markedly between Years 10 and 11. The rise between the two years (in the case of this category 'any kind of truancy in the last half term' of the order of 11 per cent) is one of the key findings. Notable also here is that by far the largest category of truanting is the mixed one: pupils who engage both in PRT and BT. Chart A presents a distribution of truants between the three categories, this time undifferentiated between Years 10 and 11; but in this instance it uses *all truants* as its base. It reveals the overwhelming preponderance of the category 'both PRT and BT.'

This is not surprising. Though the two forms of behaviour are conceptually distinct in some ways, there is a massive overlap. As we shall see later, PRT is more sensitive than is BT to curricular questions. By curricular sensitivity we mean, broadly, like or dislike of subjects/lessons, though this report leaves the conceptual distinctions between 'curriculum' and 'pedagogy', 'subject' and 'lesson' largely unprobed. Interestingly we shall also see later that long-term BT relates increasingly to dislike of particular lessons. It is true that in-depth interviewing might reveal different causes from the information gleaned from the questionnaire responses, but throughout this survey we have necessarily been constrained by those responses.

For the moment Table Four returns specifically to PRT, this time dividing it into its two sub-types and including the BT data for purposes of comparison.

Table Four
Percentages of truanting by type of truancy

Base: all pupils

	Year 10 %	Year 11 %
PRT cutting lessons	21	25
PRT leaving the building	8	13
BT	19	21

Notable here is the relative stability of BT, and a more marked increase in the case of PRT, especially in the form of leaving the building. All three types rise in Year 11 above their levels in Year 10. But PRT and leaving the building are up the most, whilst BT is up the least. It may be that the forms of truancy are converging a little in Year 11. After all, PRT and leaving the building is conceptually closer to BT than is PRT and remaining in school. It remains true that on-site PRT is still the largest

Chart A
Post registration/Blanket truancy

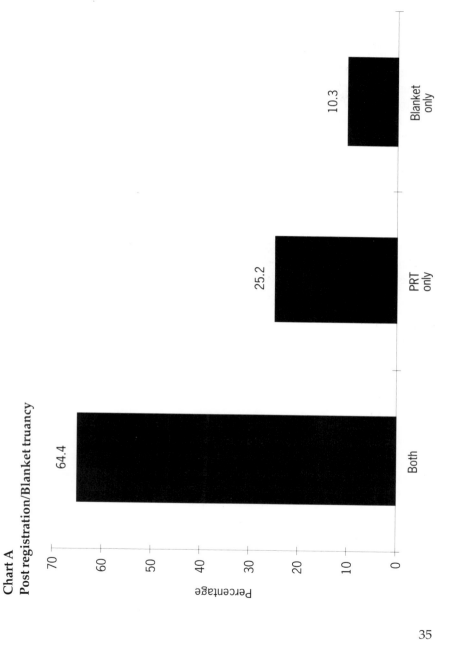

category, and noteworthy that the incidence of PRT is much greater than that of BT.

It is important to stress again that the true levels are higher than the measured ones (in any case high) because of methodological difficulties in interviewing truants, especially in the case of frequent truants. But the data available show that truancy levels are particularly high for Year 11 pupils. This is a very worrying aspect for the crucial year of certification, a year which points forward either directly to work, or indirectly to work via Sixth Form study, Further Education and/or Higher Education. This year is the last one of compulsory schooling, rounded off by important examinations. A certain disquiet can be felt in fact of the evidence that the academic purposes of the curriculum on offer are being in part rejected by a large minority of pupils.

In Table Five we have the percentages of all children who admit to any kind of truancy, shown separately for Years 10 and 11, and separately for boys and girls.

Table Five
Percentage of boys and girls truanting (any type)

Base: all pupils

	Yes	No	Total
	%	%	%
Boys Year 10	24.6	75.4	100
Girls Year 10	25.5	74.5	100
Boys Year 11	37.7	62.3	100
Girls Year 11	30.5	69.5	100

These results also appear in Chart B.

Both boys and girls, it seems, truant more in Year 11; but the increase is particularly marked in the case of boys, who move from truanting slightly less than girls in Year 10, to much more than girls in Year 11. Later in the text there is further discussion of differences in truancy between boys and girls.

Differences in truancy levels between schools[3]

The problem, we have noted, can also be approached from the point of view of schools' differing successes in securing high levels of attendance.

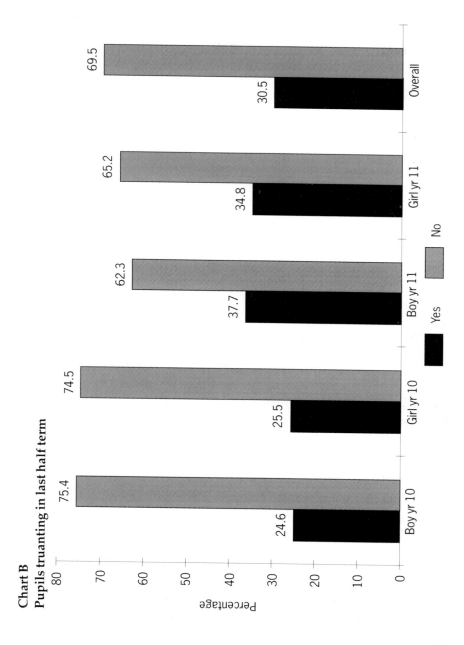

Chart B
Pupils truanting in last half term

Legend: No, Yes

Categories: Boy yr 10, Girl yr 10, Boy yr 11, Girl yr 11, Overall

Boy yr 10: 75.4 (No), 24.6 (Yes)
Girl yr 10: 74.5 (No), 25.5 (Yes)
Boy yr 11: 62.3 (No), 37.7 (Yes)
Girl yr 11: 65.2 (No), 34.8 (Yes)
Overall: 69.5 (No), 30.5 (Yes)

Percentage axis: 0, 10, 20, 30, 40, 50, 60, 70, 80

There was very considerable variation in truancy among the schools surveyed. The mean truancy level for the 150 schools in the survey is 31.0 per cent with a standard deviation of 8.3 per cent.[4]

The spread of truancy levels among schools for Years 10 and 11 is shown in Table Six.

Table Six
The spread of truancy levels among schools in Years 10 and 11 (combined)

Percentage who truanted	Schools
15% or less	3
>15% to 20%	11
>20% to 25%	23
>25% to 30%	30
>30% to 35%	42
>35% to 40%	18
>40% to 45%	16
>45% to 50%	6
More than 50%	1
Total	150

These figures reveal very considerable differences. Of our 150 schools, only three recorded levels below 15 per cent, while only seven recorded levels above 45 per cent. Ninety five schools, i.e. almost two thirds of the total, recorded levels in the range of 20 per cent plus, up to 35 per cent. On the other hand, sixteen schools, i.e. just over 10 per cent, fell into the category of more than 40 per cent to 45 per cent. It should be remembered that the data in this table could conceal very real differences in hard core levels of truancy. For the sample of schools as a whole, the undermeasurement built into the results by the absence of truants on the survey days is as real as for the aggregate percentages of truants in the pupil sample. But an individual school's result in Table Six might also make its truancy levels seem worse than they really are. While the responses of the pupil correspondents are not a question of a large amount of occasional truancy combined with very little higher frequency truancy, the results for any individual school might well be. It does not follow, then, from the more than 50 per cent level of admitted truancy in one school in Table Six, that that school has also a lot of hard core truancy. The descending scale of the table should be approached with some degree of caution.

Levels of truancy in schools in Years 10 and 11 (separated)

1. Year 10:

The mean truancy level for year 10 is 25.8 per cent with a standard deviation of 9.6 per cent.[5] The spread of truancy levels among schools for Year 10 is shown in Table Seven.

Table Seven
The spread of truancy levels among schools in Year 10

Percentage who truanted	Schools
15% or less	14
>15% to 20%	34
>20% to 25%	28
>25% to 30%	25
>30% to 35%	21
>35% to 40%	14
>40% to 45%	8
>45% to 50%	5
More than 50%	1
Total	150

Comparison of Tables Six and Seven shows that levels in Year 10 are cosiderably below the mean levels for Years 10 and 11 combined.

2. Year 11:

The mean truancy level for Year 11 is 36.5 per cent with a standard deviation of 11 per cent.[6] The spread of truancy levels among schools for Year 11 is shown in Table Eight.

Table Eight
The spread of truancy levels among schools in Year 11

Percentage who truanted	Schools
15% or less	3
>15% to 20%	7
>20% to 25%	15
>25% to 30%	21
>30% to 35%	18
>35% to 40%	27
>40% to 45%	28
>45% to 50%	13
More than 50%	18
Total	150

Comment on differences between Years 10 and 11

As can be seen by comparison of Tables Seven and Eight, there is a difference between mean truancy levels in Years 10 and 11 of over 10 per cent. This gives only part of the picture. The correlation coefficient between the percentage levels of truancy in the two years is 0.34. This is significant, but rather less than might be expected. Year 10 truancy levels turn out to be rather weak predictors of levels in Year 11. Moreover, there are large variations within schools.

In twenty eight schools (19 per cent) Year 10 levels are higher than Year 11 levels. This countertrend tends to mask overall the extent of the difference between the two levels. In sixty six schools (44 per cent) the Year 11 level is at least half as high again as the Year 10 level. Nor are these schools starting from a low Year 10 base. Sixty three of these sixty six schools (42 per cent) have Year 11 levels of truancy greater than 25 per cent, and forty four of them (29 per cent) have Year 11 levels greater than 36.5 per cent (the mean truancy level for Year 11).

In thirty one schools (21 per cent) the Year 11 level is at least double the Year 10 level.

The above figures exclude schools where the Year 10 truancy level is high enough effectively to rule out the possibility of a large increase in Year 11. The full measure of the problem is given in the fact that 112 schools in the sample (75 per cent) either have Year 11 levels half as high again as Year 10 levels or have Year 10 levels of 30 per cent or more.

Only eighteen schools (12 per cent) have both Year 10 and Year 11 levels below 25 per cent and just five schools (3 per cent) have both levels below 20 per cent. It may be inferred that many schools have difficulty in holding some of their pupils, and that the problem increases rather dramatically between Years 10 and 11.

This said, we need to take a closer look at the truancy figures, given that the measure our discussion has turned on till now is the large category who 'have truanted once in the last half term'. Even occasional acts of truancy may be insupportable to some school administrations. All, presumably, would be anxious if it could be said of pupils in their jurisdictions that they were truanting both often and in large numbers. What, then, is the real picture which emerges from our survey's findings? Is it a matter of repeated rejection of this or that aspect of school life by considerable numbers of pupils, or only of infrequent acts, which may not cause especially great anxiety among parents, heads and Local Education Authorities?

Is truancy really a problem on closer inspection?

Given that the overall levels of truancy found include large numbers of students who truant rarely, we are constrained to ask whether the problem remains a 'problem' when it is broken down.

In fact the evidence reveals a good deal of truanting in addition to the category 'once in the last half term', especially in the case of PRT; though 'once in the last half term' i.e. less than once a month, does remain the largest category. Using the base 'all pupils who completed the relevant parts of the questionnaire' (37,451), we can read off from Table Two (page 31), dealing with truancy of any type, that 1.5 per cent of all pupils truant every day; that 4.7 per cent of them truant at least 2–4 times a week; that 8.2 per cent truant at least once a week; that 13.6 per cent truant 2–3 times a month and so on.

These results indicate a worrying loss of resources and effort. On inspection, the problem is magnified, not dispelled. The conclusion can be fortified by more detailed inspection of the data coming from pupils who say they have truanted.

Examination of Tables Nine and Ten below also brings out again the fact that PR truants more often than not do not leave school. Resources can be wasted on a large scale without pupils' even leaving the building. This suggests the need for more research into on-site and off-site PRT.

There is a clear rise in the frequency of PRT between the two years. Only the hard core of every-day truants remains unchanged. In any case, here in Table Nine and in Tables Ten and Eleven following, we may be sceptical of results which show some hard core figures stable or in decline.

Table Nine
Post registration truants cutting lessons

Base: all truants

Q2a. In the last half term how often have you skipped lessons?

	Year 10 %	Year 11 %	All %
Every day	2.3	2.3	2.3
2–4 times a week	7.1	7.7	7.5
Once a week	7.9	10.9	9.6
2–3 times a month	11.6	15.4	13.7
Once a month	11.7	12.5	12.2
Less often	39.4	37.7	38.3
Never	19.9	13.5	16.3

True, we are formally restricted to the data – evidence we have in the form of what pupils say they do. This is a circumstance, however, where judicious conjecture is entirely appropriate. It seems highly likely that, of the pupils absent on the day of the survey, there was an unrepresentatively higher proportion of the children in the high frequency groups. The more children truant, the more they are likely to be absent when you want to ask them if they do so. It is logically possible that for some categories of truant, numbers are stable or falling. The more likely possibility is that levels appear to be going down because there is an increase in the rates of truancy of such offenders, and that this shows up as a decrease or a stability in the numbers of offenders in the result. For a (speculative) example, let us suppose that every-day PR truants increase the number of classes they cut. This makes it more likely that they will miss your survey. Their numbers may thus appear stable or declining when in reality they are increasing.

In any case, in Table Nine above, there are hefty increases in the 'Once a week' and '2–3 times a month' categories. Especially worthy of note is the fall between Years 10 and 11 in the 'Never' category. This category, given that the base is 'all truants', is the group of pupils whose unjustified absence is always in the form of BT. This fall in the 'Never' category shows the exponents of BT starting to engage in PRT as well.

It seems likely in the case of Table Ten that the small decline in every day truancy between the two years is actually a function of the rising

Table Ten
Post registration truants leaving the building

Base: all truants

Q3a. In the last half term how often have you registered and then left the building?

	Year 10 %	Year 11 %	All %
Every day	2.4	2.1	2.3
2–4 times a week	3.1	3.9	3.6
Once a week	4.0	4.9	4.6
2–3 times a month	4.2	5.7	5.0
Once a month	5.8	6.4	6.1
Less often	18.3	20.3	19.4
Never	62.2	56.7	58.9

rate of offences. Also, as noted above, PRT seems very much more predicated on lesson absence than on leaving the school building. The where and the what of this need further research. In any case most of the observable frequencies rise between the two years. Even were it true that slightly fewer hard core every-day exponents of PRT now leave the building, all the other categories are up, except for 'Never'. This last change indicates an increase in the numbers of exclusively BT pupils who begin to practise PRT as well in Year 11.

In Table Eleven we consider the changes between Years 10 and 11 also in the case of BT.

Table Eleven
Blanket truants and their frequency

Q4a. In the last half term how often have you not come to school at all when you were supposed to?

Base: all truants

	Year 10 %	Year 11 %	All %
Every day	2.7	2.0	2.3
2–4 times a week	6.0	5.4	5.7
Once a week	6.6	7.5	7.2
2–3 times a month	10.5	12.9	11.9
Once a month	11.9	13.0	12.6
Less often	33.9	31.8	32.6
Never	28.4	27.4	27.8

Here we find again the interesting and apparently contradictory result that the numbers of hard core offenders (every day and 2–4 times a week) have gone down somewhat between the two Years. This is probably because hard core offenders are increasing their rates of offence, though the decision to truant may well have switched to PRT. But all the other categories reveal more BT than before. For example, there is a clear move upwards (2.4 per cent) in the category 2–3 times a month.

Unfortunately there is no simple way of combining the three individual measures of frequency of truancy – BT, PRT where the truant stays on site, and PRT where the truant leaves the building. We continue to run up against the now much-laboured point that there are truants who were not there when we administered the questionnaries. In all three categories (PRT/left the premises in Table Nine, PRT/did not leave the building in Table Ten, and BT in Table Eleven) the smallest category is of the most frequent truants, and the largest category the least frequent. Though we have amply stressed the likelihood that we are getting only a subset of the evidence of frequent truancy, the problem will repay still further reflection.

Let us consider. There is a small group only who say they truant every day, of whom we probably recorded a subset. In the case of Table Eleven for example, it is useful to probe into what is implied by a pupil's admitting to BT truancy at least once a day. In the event 2.3 per cent of truants did admit to this scale of BT. By definition in a two registration day, claiming to engage in BT daily implies being absent for at least half the week. Inevitably we are going to miss many of these half-day offenders. Moreover, if, as seems probable, there is considerable all-day BT, at times mounting to several days a week, and if we are right that we missed many of these pupils, then we can assume that the real level of daily BT is very much larger than the 2.3 per cent on which we have direct data.

We probably missed many pupils who truant 2–4 times a week according to the three measures. On lower frequency (once a week, once a month, etc.) our results are more reliable. Even so, a pupil who says he or she offends 2–4 times a week on two or more of the measures, may effectively be an every day truant.

Let us, by the purest stipulation, suggest that we count as a hard core truant any pupil who says he or she truants at least once a week. Even on the data we have actually gathered from what the children say they do, the scale of the problem is considerable, as will be seen from Table Twelve.

Table Twelve
Truants who say they truant at least once a week
Base: all truants

	Daily %	2–4 times per week %	once per week %	total %
BT	2.3	5.7	7.2	15.2
PRT cutting lessons	2.3	7.5	9.6	19.4
PRT leaving building	2.3	3.6	4.6	10.5

It is noteworthy that, as in Table Three, Table Twelve suggests that PRT is a larger problem than BT. Moreover, if we consider the educational implications of Tables Nine, Ten and Eleven, they would be weighty even if some of our data as presented were not, in all probability, severe underestimations. The level of lost lessons, with all the waste of time and resources which is implied, is actually greater in the case of the hard core than in the case of those truanting minimally. In the case of Table Eleven, for example, of 11,493 truants 2.3 per cent confess to engaging in BT every day. Even if this meant only half a day at a time, this would imply two and a half days per week. Assuming a six period day, across a half term of six weeks some ninety lessons would be lost. Thus 2.3 per cent truants (264) pupils would account for 23,760 lost lessons.

The much larger category of truants engaging in BT once in a half term (32.6 per cent i.e. 3,747 pupils) account for only 11,241 lost lessons. The comparison is shown in Table Thirteen.

Table Thirteen
Comparison of lessons lost by most frequent and least frequent BT

	Lessons lost
Every-day Blanket Truants	23,760
Once a half term Blanket Truants	11,241

This result in all likelihood understates very considerably the educational and resource costs of the hard core problem. As we noted above, the numbers confessing to every-day BT are almost certainly only a subset of those engaging in it. Moreover, our assumption of only half the working week lost per hard core Blanket Truant is probably too low. We probably picked up only a small proportion of BT hard core devotés, especially if BT mostly involves whole days, singly or continuously, rather than being committed in half days, and especially if this hard core are truanting more frequently. Finally, the destruction to cumulative learning is manifestly worse in the case of frequent than in the case of occasional, truancy.

A reconsideration of the contents of Table Nine leads to similar conclusions *vis à vis* PRT. There 2.3 per cent of 11,493 truants (264) say they engage in PRT (on site) once a day. This means that even if they miss only one lesson a day (a most unlikely possibility), then across a six week period they will miss 30 lessons. This in turn implies that every-day PRT without leaving the premises, accounts for a total lesson loss per half-term of 7,920.

The largest category of PRT pupils not leaving the building, is 38.3 per cent of total truants, i.e. 4,402 pupils. These truanted only once per half term, by definition missing 4,402 lessons. This comparison is laid out in Table Fourteen.

Table Fourteen
Comparison of lessons lost by most frequent and least frequent on-site PRT

	Lessons lost
Every day PRT	7,920
Once a half term PRT	4,402

It needs to be borne in mind that this initial result understates the magnitude by which lesson loss from hard core PRT leads to greater lesson loss than does occasional PRT. In the first place we are bound to have missed some of the hard core offenders. In the second it is most unlikely that they restricted their absences to one lesson a day only.

Thus in the cases both of hard core PRT and of BT, the hard core clearly misses more lessons than do occasional truants. Our methodological constraints also mean we are likely to miss many hard core truants. Real levels are thus likely to be higher than those we found. There is no conclusive argument which can be brought against those who deny that truancy levels are higher among absentees than among those present; but such a position effectively denies the existence of a hard core problem. The evidence available suggests that the *numbers* of occasional truants increase between Years 10 and 11, while in the case of hard core truants both their numbers and their *rate of truancy* increase.

Tightening up the controls, perhaps through the construction of a tougher minatory apparatus, might touch only the large number of occasional truants, leaving the chronic hard core unaffected. On the other hand, the development of a more effective ethos in schools might drastically curtail both. We do not know.

Notes and references

1. The most common contradiction lay in respondents' claiming to have truanted and then denying this in the filling in of answer boxes. The research team decided to exclude all such contradictory responses. This makes little effective difference, since there were remarkably little ambiguous data (about 2 per cent). This is a tribute to the conduct of the field research. The critical base 'all pupils', i.e. all respondents, is merely reduced to 37,451.

2. This is a real deficiency, but one that, given the nation-wide character of the survey required of us as a condition of grant, proved impossible to remedy, on grounds of expense. Within the budget, going for a large sample required the use of one-off questionnaires. Questionnaires have undoubted advantages when numbers are large: reliability and consistency, for example. But in our case, when the problem we were investigating was partly frustrated by examples in point, the drawback is evident. Thus methodological problems were interwoven with the financial constraints. It was not satisfactory to return to administer questionnaires to pupils missing on the day of our visit. The danger of contamination by pupils who had filled in the questionnaire was apparent. Moreover, it was not clear that the worst and most chronic truants would be there to fill in the questionnaire on the day chosen for second visits. Nor did it seem satisfactory to ask hard-pressed teachers to act in our stead.

Probaly the best instrument for investigating chronic truancy would be some kind of in-depth interview. Here the researcher would concentrate on qualitative elucidation of the attitudes of frequent absentees from schools or lessons, building up a detailed profile. This is not the central stuff of large-scale research such as ours, though it would have been good to have done some such work as a qualitative assist. This was simply not feasible, however, either administratively or financially.

3. The spread of truancy levels for schools fits a normal distribution and this is assumed where standard deviations and confidence intervals are given.

4. If this result is extrapolated to all schools, then a 95 per cent confidence interval for the mean truancy level in schools is between 29.7 per cent and 32.4 per cent. About two thirds (68 per cent) of all schools should have truancy levels between 22.7 per cent and 39.3 per cent, and 96 per cent of all schools should have levels betwen 14.4 per cent and 47.4 per cent.

5. If this result is extrapolated to all schools then a 95 per cent confidence interval for the mean truancy level in schools is between 24.3 per cent and 27.4 per cent. About two thirds of all schools should have Year 10 truancy levels between 16.2 per cent and 35.4 per cent and 96 per cent of all schools have levels between 6 per cent and 45 per cent.

6. If this result is extrapolated to all schools then a 95 per cent confidence interval for the mean truancy level is between 34.7 and 38.2 per cent. About two thirds of all schools should have Year 11 truancy levels betwen 25.5 and 47.5 and 96 per cent of all schools levels between 14.5 per cent and 58.5 per cent.

4 Children's reasons for truanting

There is a long and unresolved debate in education theory and research on the proper explanation of the sources of school behaviour as this is shaped by the institution itself or by the background of pupils. None of the leading researchers today is likely to say that truancy is typically to be explained *entirely* by school factors, or alternatively by the personal aspects of individual pupils. The data uncovered in this research point both ways, but more consistently in the direction of institutional explanations. This proposition seems hopeful, at least in the sense that it is easier to work on improving schools than it is to work on improving homes and backgrounds.

Nevertheless, the difficulties are very grave. To begin with, the picture is very complex. In particular our results point both to the pre-eminence of rejection of particular lessons as a reason for truancy, and to the acceptance of the curriculum as worthwhile by most pupils. This acceptance also embraces most confessed truants, even if less closely than is the case with their non-truanting peers. Thus there is little evidence of widespread, outright hostility to the world of school. On the other hand, as we shall see in Chapter Five which deals, among other things, with children's reasons for not truanting, and again in Chapter Seven, which deals with the thorny question of 'ethos', there is also a great deal of evidence of ambivalence on the part of a large minority of pupils. Schools do not seem notably successful in getting pupils to internalise the intellectual aspects of their purposes. There is an unsatisfactory reliance on the minatory aspects of school control, rather than a genuinely successful transmission of academic consensus among the pupil body.

Our central concern here is why pupils in Years 10 and 11 truant, according to their own accounts. Our data suggest that the most important source of truancy is the school curriculum itself. Since the concept of curriculum is contestable, however, initially we need to say what we mean by it. Like many of our central educational concepts, curriculum has often been hard to define. Such concepts are both stipulative and shifting in character, though they may be nonetheless real and influential. Under the impact of the National Curriculum and its demands, for example, the concept has acquired a narrow and restricted meaning recently. It now means mostly what it used to mean before the rise of education theory. It is now the set of subjects – compulsory or optional – on offer. The question whether a school has a satisfactory 'curriculum' now asks mostly whether it handles satisfactorily the demands of the National Curriculum. If our report says that we believe that truancy is more than anything else a curricular phenomenon, it is this newly re-narrowed meaning which we imply. Our research has not attempted any distinction between 'lessons' and 'subjects'.

Our evidence is consistent with the view that the rejection of lessons plays a central part in some pupils' decisions to truant. About two thirds of all truants say they engage in truancy in order to avoid particular lessons. This means that about one in five of ALL pupils truant from particular lessons. Responding to Q5b, 67 per cent of truants say they truant because of a particular lesson or lessons. This is a key result, laid out, together with Q5a, Q5b and Q5c in Table Fifteen.

Table Fifteen
Reasons given for truanting (avoidance of school, avoidance of lessons and other reasons)

Base: all truants

Q5a. In the last half term have you ever not come to school when you were supposed to, or left school after registration, because you did not like school?

Q5b. In the last half term have you ever not come to school when you were supposed to, or left school after registration, or skipped a lesson because you wanted to miss a particular lesson?

Q5c. In the last half term have you ever not come to school when you were supposed to, or left school after registration, or skipped lessons for any other reason?

	All truants %	PRT only %	BT only %	PRT&BT %
To avoid school	49	27	35	60
To avoid lessons	67	68	40	74
Other reasons	45	31	39	54

Note that the wish to avoid lessons is the most powerful motive for truancy, especially in the case of PRT. With pupils who engage only in

PRT the margin is huge; but it is large also in the case of pupils who do both and quite marked even in the case of pupils who engage only in BT, though in their case other reasons are almost as important.

It is not that there is no considerable opinion against school among truants. Clearly there is. In so far as pupils are able, however, to distinguish the idea of liking/disliking school from the related idea of liking/disliking lessons, it is apparent that on their own accounts far more locate their decisions to truant in lesson-dissatisfaction than in general dislike of school. As we shall argue below, our questionnaire was probably partly at fault, in that its three-item Q5 had its component ideas too tightly packed for some of the students to separate them out effectively.

Dislike of school and lessons are mixed into each other in the answers given, but dislike of particular lessons predominates. Forty nine per cent of truants said they truanted partly or wholly because they did not like school. Many of these pupils, however, responded in answer to Q5a, that they truant at least partly as a reaction to particular lessons or how they are delivered, as may be seen in Table Sixteen.

Table Sixteen
Reasons given for dislike of school

Bases: all truants and truants who truant because of dislike of school

Q5a. In the last half term have you ever not come to school when you were supposed to, or left school after registration, because you did not like school?

	(1) All truants %	(2) Truants who truant because of dislike of school %
School boring/oppressive	11	23
Particular lesson boring/oppressive	10	20
School work too hard	4	9
Dislike of teachers	13	27
Already in trouble/detention	1	2

It will be seen among both groups of pupils that the biggest reasons for disliking school itself have a large lesson component and an even larger element of personal antipathy to teachers. These two elements of dislike of lessons and teachers loom larger in dislike of school in the case of pupils who truant, they say, because of dislike of school, than among truants as a whole.

It may be that the close proximity of questions in the case of the subdivided Q5 causes truanting respondents not to distinguish clearly between 'school' and 'lessons', and that the 49 per cent (Table Fifteen) is rather misleading. Certainly when asked in a more isolated way whether they like school, truants came nowhere near this high percentage (See Table 32 in the next chapter and Table Seventeen and its discussion below).

The point about the lessons looming large in pupils' reasons for truancy is demonstrable even more clearly if we consider pupils separated between those saying they had only one reason for truanting, and those claiming a mixture of reasons. This is laid out in Table Seventeen.

Table Seventeen
Unique versus mixed reasons for truanting

Base: all truants

	All truants %	PRT only %	BT only %	PRT&BT %
To avoid lessons only	19	30	13	20
To avoid school only	5	4	8	4
For other sole reasons	7	6	11	6
Mixture of reasons	69	60	68	70

It is notable that almost a fifth of truants say they truant for no other reason than to avoid particular lessons. Those who claim they do it exclusively to avoid school are by comparison very few in number. The preponderance of lesson avoidance is especially marked in the case of PRT. Avoidance of school, by contrast, does not show up strongly in any category. This would seem to strengthen our contention that school is not notably an unpopular institution with its constrained denizens.

Of all these truants we find in Table Eighteen below that 14 per cent say they truanted (partly or wholly) because they disliked a particular lesson. Twenty per cent truanted (partly or wholly) because they thought a particular lesson was in some way irrelevant. Nine per cent said that a lesson (or lessons) was too difficult and 8 per cent truanted because of not completing coursework or homework. Twenty seven per cent of these pupils cited teacher unpleasantness as a reason for truanting. Interestingly, however, only 2 per cent said that teachers were unhelpful and only 1 per cent that teachers were not interested – an encouraging finding.

These decisions for truanting, broadly described as 'curricular' or 'pedagogic', are shown in Table Eighteen. They are not separate categories of reason, since some truants answered more than one affirmatively.

Table Eighteen
Curricular and pedagogic reasons for truanting from lessons
Base: all truants

	%
The lesson is not enjoyable	14
The lesson is irrelevant	20
The lesson is too difficult	9
Homework or coursework have not been finished	8
The teacher is unpleasant	27
The teacher is unhelpful	2
The teacher is not interested	1

Some truants will have given more than one of the above answers, so the percentages cannot be simply summed to give an overall picture. It is clear that a great many children reject particular facets of the school (particular subjects in the curriculum or the homework or coursework which goes with them, or the people who teach them) rather than the institution as a whole. As we saw in Table Sixteen, even among those pupils who said they truant to avoid school, only 23 per cent stated that school was oppressive, depressing or dull. Moreover, in Table Seventeen we found that only 5 per cent of truants gave general dislike of school as a unique reason for their truancy.

More frequent truancy is more subject-sensitive

Worries about subjects are a rising function of truancy, as revealed in Tables Nineteen, Nineteen A and Nineteen B. Amongst frequent truants, 81 per cent of Post Registration truants who absent themselves once a week or more, say this is to avoid a particular lesson. Among frequent perpetrators BT too is much more sensitive to subjects. Seventy eight per cent of Blanket truants saying they truant 2–3 times a month or more, say this is to avoid particular lessons. In Table Fifteen, we found PRT for purposes of lesson avoidance at 68 per cent only, and BT for the same purposes at 40 per cent only. In Table Nineteen A we find that PRT for this motive jumps significantly at higher frequency and that BT in this regard nearly doubles. This suggests an increasingly common motivation for PRT and BT once the latter reaches a sufficient level. First, however, in Table Nineteen we present those answers where pupils said that they truanted wholly or partly to avoid school.

Table Nineteen
Frequency of truanting (partly or wholly because of school)

Base: all truants

Q5a. In the last half term have you ever not come to school when you were supposed to, or left school after registration because you did not like school?

	BT only %	PRT only %	BT&PRT %
Once a week or more	62	42	70
Once a month or more but less than once a week	52	33	54
Less than once a month	37	21	32

With greater frequency of truanting, for all three categories, we find an accompanying greater alienation from school. We return, however, to our claim that lessons are more important. Table Nineteen A, for example, lays out the percentages of truants claiming that their decisions were wholly or partly to avoid lessons.

Table Nineteen A
Frequency of truanting (partly or wholly) to avoid lessons

Base: all truants

Q5b. In the last half term have you ever not come to school when you were supposed to, or left school after registration, or skipped a lesson because you wanted to miss a particular lesson?

	BT only %	PRT only %	BT&PRT %
Once a week or more	66	75	80
Once a month or more but less than once a week	69	75	75
Less than once a month	54	64	59

Table Nineteen B, on the other hand, lays out the percentages of truants saying they truanted for other reasons that the wish to avoid school or lessons.

54

Table Nineteen B
Frequency of truanting (partly or wholly) because of other reasons

Base: all truants

Q5c. In the last half term have you ever not come to school when you were supposed to, or left school after registration, or skipped lessons for any other reason?

	BT only %	PRT only %	BT&PRT %
Once a week or more	52	36	58
Once a month or more but less than once a week	50	37	50
Less than once a month	41	26	37

Comment on Tables Nineteen, Nineteen A and Nineteen B

These tables (Nineteen, Nineteen A and Nineteen B) in each case were compiled on the basis that the truants said they truanted only, or also, to miss school (Table Nineteen), lessons (Table Nineteen A), or for some other reason (Table Nineteen B). All three explanations are clearly important; but comparison of the tables shows that the wish to avoid lessons is the single largest factor, and other reasons than the desire to miss school or lessons, the weakest factor. Desire to avoid lessons is stronger for all three categories of truants (BT, PRT, and BT & PRT) at all three frequencies, than any other reason. This wish to avoid lessons starts at higher percentages in the lowest of the three frequencies and also rises to higher percentages in the highest of the three frequencies, than is the case with the other two reasons given for truanting. The inference is that while truants act as they do for a number of reasons, the wish to avoid lessons is the strongest explanation they give, and this is especially so for frequent truants. It is also apparent that while BT does occur in order to avoid lessons, increasingly as its frequency rises, it is nevertheless less predicated on lesson avoidance than PRT or PRT & BT.

The data revealed in Tables Nineteen, Nineteen A, and Nineteen B, clearly confound the view that truancy is due to factors over which schools have little or no control. If lessons were better regarded by truants, levels of truancy would fall. After all, most pupils do not truant and most truants attend most of their lessons. It would not seem beyond the power of schools to reduce their truancy levels.

Thus we have powerful evidence that truancy is primarily a response to lessons seen as unsatisfactory. More precisely, some kind of lesson-dissatisfaction is a more significant factor than any other. Two thirds of truants say they truant to avoid specific lessons (see Table Fifteen). Let us repeat a key statistic: one in five of *all* pupils truant because they want to miss particular lessons. This leads naturally to a discussion of individual subjects. Our research has uncovered evidence of pupils' dislike of lessons, of subjects themselves, of teaching methods and of the personalities of teachers. Unfortunately, we have not been able to rank these influences on the decision to truant. 'Lesson-dissatisfaction' remains an amorphous category.

Truancy and individual subjects

The raw figures suggest that Maths (22 per cent), English (21 per cent) and PE/Games (21 per cent) are the most unpopular subjects, with History (9 per cent) and other subjects faring relatively well. This result is a little misleading. Some subjects are compulsory, some are options. Not all students study all subjects. This will yield a misleadingly low level of truancy for less popular (i.e. less studied) subjects. These figures are shown in Table Twenty. In each case here, the percentages shown as truanting from different subjects are taken from the category 'truanted to avoid particular subjects'. They are *not* percentages of those studying particular subjects who truant from them.

Table Twenty
Truancy percentages from selected subjects
Base: all truants from the category 'truanted to avoid particular lessons'

	%
Maths	22
English	21
PE/Games	21
French	18
Science	18
Geography	9
History	9
RE	7
Technology	3

In fact a better indicator of the comparative truancy level in various subjects is given if the base in the case of each is the number of truants who actually study that subject. This is shown in Table Twenty One. We may take the case of Geography. In Table Twenty we saw that 9 per cent of all truants from the category 'truanted to avoid particular lessons' said they truanted from Geography among other subjects. In Table Twenty One, of those truants who study Geography, 16 per cent said they truanted from this subject because they do not like it. This is a more accurate picture of truancy from Geography lessons.

Table Twenty One
Truants on the grounds of dislike of subject
Base: for each subject all truants who study it

	%
Maths	19
English	18
PE/Games	34
French	27
Science	19
Geography	16
History	19
RE	20
Technology	16

The marked unpopularity of PE/Games and French is notable here. The divergence between truancy levels for 'compulsory' subjects like Maths and English as between the two tables Twenty and Twenty One is due simply to the differences in the bases used. The difference in the case of PE/Games between the two tables suggests that *de facto* this subject is not 'compulsory'.

Reasons given for truanting

There is quite a wide range of reasons for truanting from various lessons. The main examples of these are shown in Table Twenty Two.

Thirty six per cent of truants aiming to avoid particular lessons say that the lesson they truant from is irrelevant. Almost a quarter of all truants make the same suggestion. As it happens three of the four of the most cited reasons for truanting from lessons are lesson-predicated, involving questions of the relevance, inherent appeal and evaluation of subject-matter. The claim of the irrelevance of lessons, in particular, is arresting. The vocabulary argues a widespread presence in the school population of

Table Twenty Two
Reasons given for avoiding lessons

Bases: all truants and truants who truant to avoid lessons

		(1) All truants	(2) Truants who truant to avoid lessons
		%	%
Irrelevant lessons	(I)	24	36
Dislike of teacher	(DT)	19	29
Dislike of subject	(DS)	15	22
Coursework problems	(C)	13	19
Difficulty of subject	(D)	9	14
Poor teaching	(PT)	2	3
Bullying	(B)	0.7	1

The same material is displayed in Chart C.

instrumental values. But the clear-cut, substantial agreement among truants over issues (I), (DT), (DS) and (C) also suggests a relatively pondered process of rational decision-making. It is strong evidence of a degree of curricular rejection among some pupils in Years 10 and 11.

Coursework is notable as contributing substantially to lesson truancy. Nineteen per cent, i.e. almost a fifth of those truanting from specific lessons, give it as a reason. Fourteen per cent give the reason that the subject is too difficult. This is sizeable, and raises questions both about the spread of ability and about the prior intellectual formation of these pupils. Such a reason for truanting might conceivably be much reduced by better earlier preparation. At the same time this figure is low enough to argue against any claim that it is overwhelmingly low achievers who truant. True, low achievers may sometimes find the work too difficult simply because they are not pushed hard. Or at times they may be pushed beyond their powers. This is conjecture. Perhaps there is institutional slackness in some cases. Were it addressed, the force of this motive for truanting might be much reduced. This possibility throws the emphasis back on school effect (roughly on ethos) rather than innate ability. Bullying, another alleged major contribution to truancy, is in fact a negligible factor at 1 per cent or 0.7 per cent, depending which category of truants we look at.

Chart C
Reasons for lesson truancy

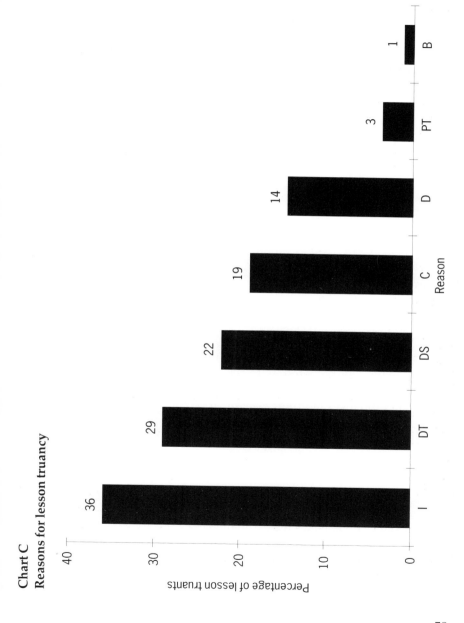

Other reasons for truanting

Table Twenty Three shows the information given by answers to Q5c – other reasons for truanting. Forty five per cent of all truants said they exclusively, or also, truanted for reasons other than a dislike of school or lessons.

Table Twenty Three
Other reasons for truanting in rank order

Bases: all truants and truants who truant for other reasons

		(1) All truants %	(2) Truants who truant for other reasons %
Other activities	(OA)	10	22
Not bothered	(NB)	6	13
Illness/feeling cold	(I/C)	4	8
General school dislike	(GS)	2.5	5
Tiredness	(T)	2.5	5
Depression	(D)	1.8	4
Home problems	(H)	1.4	3
Bullying	(B)	0.9	2
Peer pressure	(P)	0.9	2

See also Chart D.

The lure of other activities is evidently strong. Something like apathy (being 'Not bothered' with school) seems to affect some students. The other factors are all small, though collectively they may add up to a significant influence, and there is again apparently no strong overlap with dislike of school. Illness and bullying are not large problems either. Nor do home problems evidently exert much effect on what children say in their questionnaire answers, though home presumably has an enormous unconscious effect.

Truancy: An individual or a social act?

Table Twenty Three makes it clear that truancy has social dimensions. The category 'Other activities' includes meeting other people. It is also note-worthy that this explanation for truancy again suggests a choice made on rational grounds. It is apparent that truancy has social as well as individual components, as Table Twenty Four makes more emphatically clear.

Chart D
Other reasons for truanting

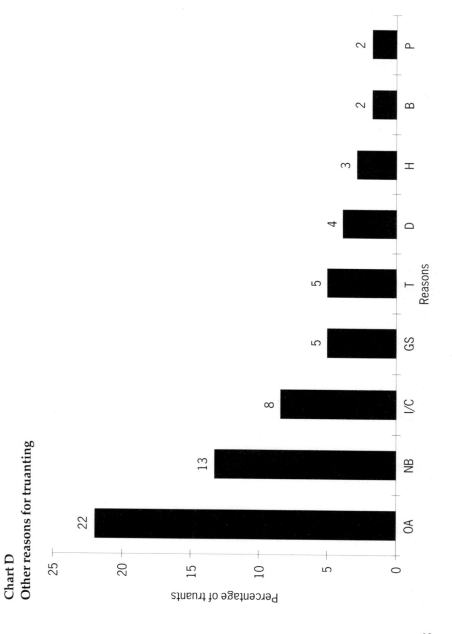

Indeed, rather few truants (15 per cent) exclusively truant alone. This does not imply, as we have seen (P in Table Twenty Three), that much pressure is put on truants by peers. The decision remains an individual one. Truancy is largely a social phenomenon, but one based on individual choice, Table Twenty Three makes it clear that peer pressure and bullying are influences, but only small ones. In other words truancy, though largely social in character, is a voluntary act. Of the sociability of truancy, on the other hand, Table Twenty Four leaves us in no doubt. Thirty six per cent of truants say they always truant with friends. Forty nine per cent say they truant both individually and with friends. Moreover truancy is widely appreciated. Sixty per cent of all children say that they know their friends have engaged in PRT.

Table Twenty Four shows this social character of truancy.

Table Twenty Four
Truancy: alone or with friends?

Base: all truants

Q9. In the last half term if you left school after registration or skipped lessons was this always alone, or always with friends or sometimes alone and sometimes with friends?

	All truants %	PRT only %	BT only %	PRT&BT %
Always alone	15	18	12	14
Always with friends	36	45	15	37
Sometimes alone and sometimes with friends	49	37	74	48

Whatever the push influence of subjects, or teachers, seen as dislikeable, it is apparent that the pull attraction of friendship is a significant motive for truancy in our secondary schools.

5 Other pupil-commentary on school

In this short chapter we are concerned with other truancy-related commentary gleaned from our respondents' answers to our questionnaires. Of central interest will be students' attitudes to the enjoyment of school in general, including the perceived usefulness or otherwise of the subjects they study; their attitudes to parental and school disapproval of truancy; the ease with which they can truant if they choose; and their intentions with regard to more education, either at school or elsewhere. Particularly important are their explanations as to why they do *not* truant.

Reasons for not truanting

The data here are ambiguous. On the one hand non-truants' declared wish not to miss school (40 per cent) was surpassed as a reason for attendance only by fear of being found out in truancy by parents (48 per cent). Worry that the school might find out (38 per cent), though substantial, weighed less. More finely graded favourable comments on the value of school were little in evidence. For example, liking lessons got only 3 per cent of votes as a reason for attending. The data are consistent (no more than this is claimed) with school's being popular socially rather than intellectually. On the other hand the large desire to be at school (40 per cent. See above) may also subsume approval of the curriculum. So ambiguity reigns, though it looks as if opinion is evenly split between non-truanting for positive reasons and for minatory reasons. Conscience is little quoted. Neither is fear of police voiced by those deterred from truanting, though both BT and PRT in its leaving the building form, might conceivably bring truants into contact with the police, nor, indeed, does fear of the Educational Welfare Service, with which our truants might more normally be expected to connect, figure in our questionnaire data. Perhaps these gaps are welcome in a free society. The main findings are shown in Table Twenty Five.

Table Twenty Five
Reasons for not truanting

Base: all non-truants

		%
Parents, Concern that parents would find out	(Pa)	48
Not miss school (do not want to)	(M)	40
School, Concern that school might find out	(S)	38
Pointless to truant	(Po)	10
Miss work (did not want to)	(W)	6
Education is important	(E)	6
Like school	(L)	3

These results are also shown in Chart E

Truancy, parents and teachers

While 48 per cent of non-truants say they would worry that their parents might find out, 44 per cent of truants say their parents know. This latter is a high figure (though obviously much smaller than the number of pupils deterred), suggesting that whatever the motivation for truancy, some parents are party to it. It is also consistent with the possibility of vigilant teachers making a fuss and reporting the offence to parents. This seems less likely. First, as we shall see later, most truants find the activity easy. Secondly, if teachers are acting in this way, it does not seem to be effective. More convincing is the claim that a high level of parent awareness also suggests a high level of condonation.

While 38 per cent of non-truants say they are deterred by the fear that their teachers might find out, exactly the same proportion of truants (again obviously a much smaller number) say their teachers do not know, while a further 30 per cent say they do know. In fact the question on teachers' knowledge of truancy on the pupil questionnaire (Question 7) provided a box for affirmative ticking only in relation to 'at least one teacher knows'. Thus a collective response in a school, however positive to the effect that teachers do know, does not mean that many of them do. Large numbers of truants in Years 10 or 11 could be referring to a few teachers or even to only one.

Nevertheless, given that 25 per cent of truants say that they do not know if teachers are aware of their truancy, we may legitimately conclude

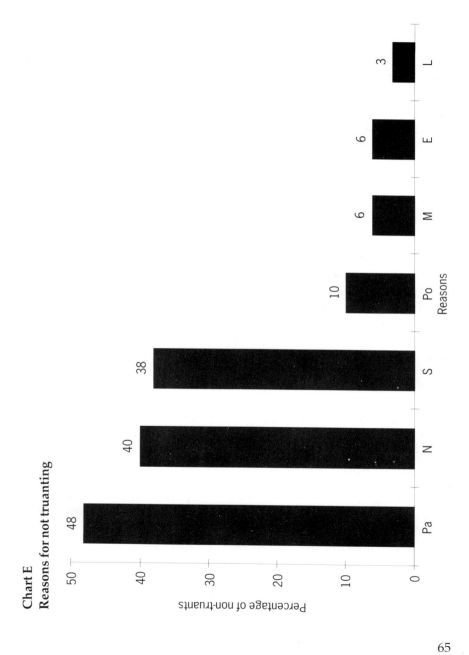

Chart E
Reasons for not truanting

Percentage of non-truants (vertical axis)

Pa 48
N 40
S 38
Po 10
M 6
E 6
L 3

Reasons (horizontal axis)

65

that teachers' awareness of truancy relates to more than 30 per cent of truants. While this will clearly remain a much smaller number of persons than those deterred by fear of teachers' displeasure, it remains a significant number and does seem to provide strong, *prima facie* evidence of a negative 'school ethos' at work. It is true that this evidence is also consistent with teachers' being on their guard against truancy. The declared ease of truancy, however (see Table Twenty Eight), points in the opposite direction and also suggests a negative ethos effect. Frankly, the figures in the case, both of parent and teacher awareness, are alarmingly high. They suggest a marked degree of failure by some homes to uphold the purposes of compulsory education and a considerable shortfall by some schools in this regard. Moreover, the notion that 38 per cent of truants think that teachers do *not* know about truancy carries its own burden of disquiet.

The figures are presented in Tables Twenty Six and Twenty Seven.

Table Twenty Six
Are parents aware of truancy?

Base: all truants

	All truants %	PRT only %	BT only %	PRT & BT %
Yes	44	35	53	47
No	36	48	24	35
Don't know	13	11	12	15
Not stated	6	7	11	4

Table Twenty Seven
Are teachers aware of truancy

Base: all truants

N.B. The question was constructed so that truants could say whether or not at least one teacher knew.

	All truants %	PRT only %	BT only %	PRT & BT %
Yes	30	27	19	34
No	38	42	46	36
Don't Know	25	24	23	26
Not stated	7	7	12	4

Truancy: easy or difficult?

The results displayed in Tables Twenty Six and Twenty Seven, depressing or otherwise, lead naturally to discussion of the general ease or difficulty of truanting. The answers given by our respondents are displayed in Table Twenty Eight.

Table Twenty Eight
Is truancy easy or difficult?

Base: all truants

	All truants %	PRT only %	BT only %	PRT & BT %
Easy	46	48	21	50
Neutral	30	33	17	32
Difficult	8	8	5	8
Don't know	17	10	57	10

It is noteworthy that PRT is seen as easier than BT by those who engage in only one of the two. Those who engage in both regard truancy as easier than is the case in either of the other two type categories and, by definition, than in the 'All' group. It should be remembered that this is the largest differentiated category of truancy and that PRT is its larger component. It may be that PRT leads to a taste for absence, which comes to seem easy and familiar. We simply do not know whether truancy starts as BT (perhaps even at the primary stage) and spills over later into PRT, or whether in secondary school the sequence is the other way round. If there are general relationships of this kind between the two main forms of truancy we do not know about them.

Overall, truancy does not appear to be seen as difficult by those who say they truant, and the largest group who say they truant also say they find it the easiest. Forty six per cent of all truants say it is easy. Those who say it is difficult are only 8 per cent. On the other hand there are many truants in all the categories who say it is neither easy nor difficult. There are some brakes on the activity, it seems. In fact, while the administrative controls on truancy are apparently not very daunting to would-be offenders, there is good evidence that such controls can significantly lessen truancy levels, as we shall see. This may reasonably balance the alarm we feel about the numbers of parents and teachers who know that pupils truant.

School and parental vigilance as deterrents to truancy

When we look at the schools in terms of the pupils who say they are *deterred*, quite a hopeful picture emerges. As we saw in Table Twenty Five, 48 per cent of non-truants fear that discovery would cause parental displeasure and 38 per cent entertain similar anxieties about school. Generally speaking, pupils who want to truant do seem to find it relatively easy. At the same time the evidence is that schools *can* deter truancy and some of them are much better at it than others. The percentage of truants who found truancy easy varied considerably between schools (from 18 per cent to 90 per cent) with a mean figure of 48 per cent and a standard deviation of 10.7. The correlation coefficient between truancy levels and this measure is 0.28. Table Twenty Nine shows this connection between ease and levels of truancy.

Table Twenty Nine
Truancy levels of schools ranked by ease of truancy

	Truancy levels %
Twenty five schools with largest percentages of truants finding truancy easy	33.7
Middle 100 schools	31.6
Twenty five schools with smallest percentages of truants finding truancy easy	26.0

School vigilance can have a considerable effect. Vigilant schools do better and it is apparent that the good effects of better than average vigilance are greater than the bad effects of worse than average vigilance. The best twenty five schools are further from the truancy level of the middle 100 than are the worst twenty five schools.

A similar overall effect can also be detected if we consider the percentage of *non-truants* who stated that a reason for not truanting was the possibility that the school might find out. The range was again large (10 per cent to 61 per cent) with a mean figure of 36.4 per cent and a standard deviation of 9.5. From this figure it seems that many pupils can be deterred from truanting by school measures. The correlation between this variable and truancy levels is –0.33, and Table Thirty illustrates the effect.

Table Thirty
Schools ranked by percentage of non-truants deterred from truanting by the possibility of school finding out

	Truancy levels %
Twenty five schools with the highest percentage of non-truants deterred	27.4
Middle 100 schools	30.7
Twenty five schools with the lowest percentage of non-truants deterred	35.8

Would be truants seem mindful of school. We may reasonably interpret our results here as indicating variations in ethos, teacher authority and punishment. Many pupils worry about teachers' displeasure. Table Thirty illustrates in particular the adverse effects on school life in the bottom twenty five schools of a high level of indifference among pupils to schools' finding out about truancy. Indeed, in this instance the effects are most marked on downward differences. The worst schools are further from the middle 100 performance than are the best.

Parental concern also has an effect on truancy levels. The percentage of non-truants who did not truant because of the possibility of discovery by parents was generally high. The mean is 46 per cent (range 19 per cent to 68 per cent), standard deviation 9.0 and the correlation between this variable and truancy levels is –0.24. This effect is shown in Table Thirty A.

Table Thirty A
Schools ranked by percentage of non-truants who are deterred from truancy by the possibility of parents finding out

	Truancy levels %
Twenty five schools with highest percentage of non-truants deterred	26.1
Middle 100 schools	31.4
Twenty five schools with lowest percentage of non-truants deterred	34.4

It is apparent that a minatory control is effective, again with the effect stronger on better performances than on weaker, as was the case in

Table Twenty Nine. The reverse effect operates in Table Thirty. Having pupils with strong regard for parents improves attendance in schools more than *not* having such pupils worsens their truancy. In any case parental and school vigilance are shown collectively to be very important in controlling levels of truancy.

The influence of non-minatory controls on the decision not to truant

It is apparent from Tables Thirty and Thirty A that teacher and parental displeasure are a significant control on the tendency to truant and that schools vary considerably in this regard. It is also apparent that most pupils endorse many of the purposes of school. Many pupils specifically say they do not want to miss school (see Table Twenty Five). Aware that most pupils like school and that a majority or truants either like or tolerate it, we now examine in Table Thirty One the question whether approval of school, i.e. an internalised approbation for various reasons, matches minatory controls as an influence deterring truancy.

Table Thirty One
Schools ranked by percentage of non-truants not wishing to miss school

	Mean truancy level %
Twenty five schools with highest percentage of pupils not wanting to miss school	31.1
Middle 100 schools	31.1
Twenty five schools with lowest percentage of pupils not wanting to miss school	30.5

It is sadly evident that the desire not to miss school has a much weaker holding effect upon potential truants than does the force of minatory controls. This does not mean, of course, that a positive desire not to miss school is not important in the life of schools. It means what it seems to mean. Human nature being what it is, at school or elsewhere, there are some pupils who will truant if they have the opportunity even when they like school, lessons and so on.

Truancy, attendance and enjoyment of school

This brings us naturally to the question of enjoyment. The survey team expected to find that most children like school. Certainly most non-truants in the survey like school. Perhaps more surprising to some people will be the revelation that most truants say they do not actively dislike it either, as we see in Table Thirty Two.

Table Thirty Two
Is school enjoyable or not?

Base: all pupils

	All truants %	Non-truants %	PRT only %	BT only %	PRT & BT %
Always enjoyable	2	3	3	3	2
Mostly enjoyable	31	47	38	39	28
Neither (neutral)	33	36	33	32	33
Mostly not	17	9	14	16	18
Never	14	4	9	7	17

These results are also depicted in Chart F.

Predictably, non-truants have a greater affection for school, but the effect is not as pronounced as might have been thought. About a third of truants surveyed find school always or mostly unenjoyable. A third are neutral and the remaining third mostly or always like school. This result will bear pejorative construction. For example, in the case of the largest category of truants, those who engage in both PRT and BT, those who find school never enjoyable number 17 per cent. Those who find it mostly not enjoyable number 18 per cent. This tallies to an alienated 35 per cent.

Even so, 28 per cent in this category find school mostly enjoyable. Much will therefore turn on what is made of the large (33 per cent) neutral group. If neutral means 'indifferent', the picture looks bleak. If it means 'accepting', the outlook is quite reasonable. As we shall see later (in Tables Thirty Three and Thirty Four), there is, compared to the responses to the question of enjoyment of school, a more clear-cut endorsement of the usefulness of school subjects. There is also an overwhelming declared intention to stay on for more education. If we accept these as modifying favourably our judgement of the interpretation of neutrality *vis a vis* enjoying school, then the top three figures in the PRT & BT column of Table

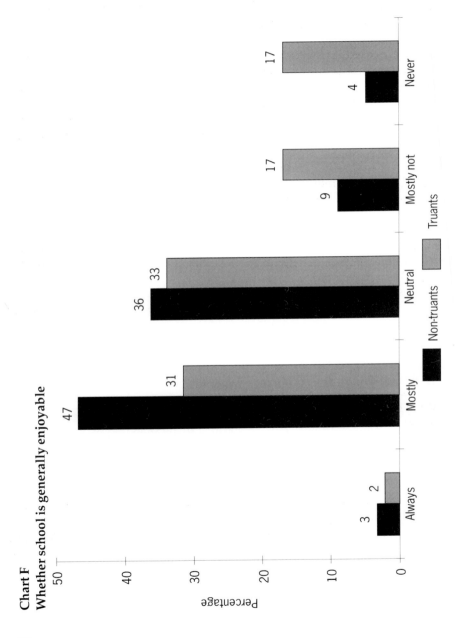

Chart F
Whether school is generally enjoyable

Thirty Two can be construed as showing 66 per cent of the largest category of truants as either liking or accepting school.

This result runs contrary to the notion that truants will be hostile to school as an institution. Only about a third of pupils surveyed are truants and only about a third of truants dislike school. This result, as we noted earlier, suggests that our contradictory responses to Q5 resulted from overpacking the question with components pupils found misleading and difficult to separate. When, as in Table Thirty Two, the question of the enjoyment of school is put in a more self-contained way, the hostility or dislike is much less apparent. It is not school but certain *lessons* about which these truants seem to have reservations. Let us recall that 67 per cent of truants are seeking to avoid particular parts of the curriculum.

Here we should see whether the enjoyment of school, seen as a phenomenon of acceptance or approbation, compares favourably with the influence of minatory controls as a deterrent to truancy. This question can be examined in the light of Table Thirty Two A.

Table Thirty Two A is constructed around the answers to Question 13 in the pupil questionnaire.

Question 13
Do you think school is:
Always enjoyable?
Mostly enjoyable?
Neither enjoyable nor unenjoyable?
Mostly not enjoyable?
Never enjoyable?

Each response was given a score from 0 for enjoying school without qualification through to 4 for not enjoying school at all. The results were averaged for each school. Thus the higher the score the less did children like school. In other words, the lower the score the lower the alienation rating.

Table Thirty Two A
Schools ranked by percentages of non-truants who enjoy school

	Mean truancy level %
Twenty five schools with best enjoyment, i.e. lowest alienation rating	30.7
Middle 100 schools	30.9
Twenty five schools with lowest enjoyment, i.e. highest alienation rating	31.5

There is very little effect visible here. As with Table Thirty One, approbation seems less effective against truancy than minatory deterrents. In Table Thirty Two A, the holding force of enjoyment of school seems weaker by far than such minatory controls. Such a result does not mean that enjoyment is not important. It does suggest that teenage behaviour is such that vigilance is required to back up the value which potential or actual truants say they put on school and lessons. The twenty five schools most enjoyed by pupils truant scarcely less than the 100 middle schools.

Usefulness of school subjects as a deterrent to truancy

Truancy clearly occurs for many reasons. In a sense the idea that it may be more than anything a curricular phenomenon, is fortified by the value truants, as well as non-truants, place on the subjects they study. It is perhaps when their expectations of usefulness are not met that pupils are most likely to consider absenting themselves from school or lessons. Table Thirty Three shows the response to Q14 and compares truants to non-truants. It reveals that over half (54 per cent) of truants think that most of what they are learning will be useful, and over three quarters (78 per cent) think that at least half of their subjects will be useful.

Not surprisingly the corresponding proportions are higher for non-truants, but again the differential is nothing like what would be the case were truants massively alienated from school.

Unfortunately, the favourable rating given to most subject-matter by pupils once again turns out not to be associated with more than slight variations in the ability of schools to combat truancy, as we see in Table Thirty Three A.

Table Thirty Three
Will school subjects be useful?

Base: all pupils

	All truants %	Non-truants %	PRT only %	BT only %	PRT & BT %
All useful	13	15	15	15	12
Mostly useful	41	56	45	47	38
About half useful	24	21	24	24	26
Only a small part useful	14	7	12	9	16
None useful	6	1	2	2	6

These findings are also reproduced in Chart G.

Table Thirty Three was constructed in response to Question 14 on the pupil questionnaire.

Question 14

Do you think what you are learning in school will be:
All useful?
Mostly useful?
About half useful?
Only a small part useful?
Not useful at all?

As with Table Thirty Two A, in Table Thirty Three A pupils in the most favourably inclined group have been scored at 0, through to the least well inclined group, who have been scored at 4. The results were then averaged.

Table Thirty Three A
Schools ranked by percentages of pupils finding what they learn useful

	Mean truancy level %
Twenty five schools with highest usefulness, i.e. lowest alienation rating	28.9
Middle 100 schools	31.6
Twenty five schools with lowest usefulness, i.e. highest alienation rating	30.5

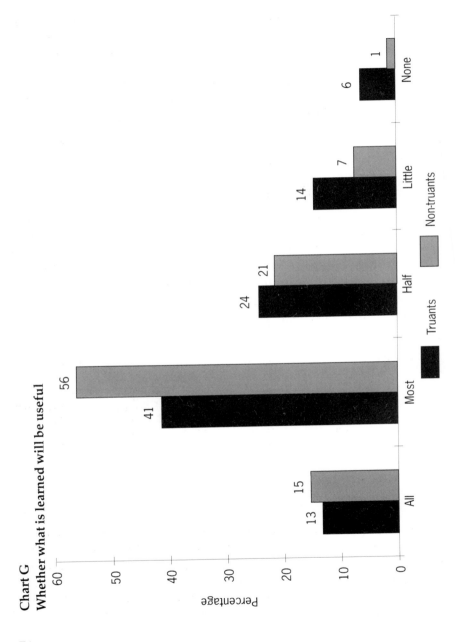

Chart G
Whether what is learned will be useful

Percentage

Non-truants

Truants

All — 13, 15
Most — 41, 56
Half — 24, 21
Little — 14, 7
None — 6, 1

It will be seen in Table Thirty Three A that the effects on truancy levels of positive and negative evaluation of the usefulness of what is learned are extremely slight. The utility rating of the weakest twenty five schools actually connects with a truancy level below that of the middle 100 schools in the utility rating. All that is apparent is some improvement effect in terms of truancy in the twenty five schools where lessons are seen as most useful. This utility question yields even slighter grounds for thinking that positive approbation of school will in itself have a large deterrent effect on truancy levels, than the itself slight influence of positive or negative verdicts on school enjoyment seen in Table Thirty Two A.

Continuing education post 16

None of these negative findings undermines the contention that school is mostly popular or tolerated. Further evidence against widespread or endemic alienation from the curriculum in general is supplied by the data uncovered on pupils' intentions to stay on. These were assembled from the answers to Q17 and appear in Table Thirty Four.

Table Thirty Four
Would you like to continue your education?

Base: All pupils

Q17. Would you like to continue with your education at school or college after you have finished the 11(5)th Year?

	All truants %	Non- truants %	PRT only %	BT only %	PRT & BT %
Yes	58	75	66	66	54
No	18.5	8.5	16.5	12	20
Don't know	25	18	22	23	26

These findings are also shown in Chart H

It is clear that truants in our survey are not in general hostile to the process of education. Over half of all truants, and two thirds of students in the categories PRT only and BT only, want to continue their education. Only 18.5 per cent of truants have definitely decided against further education. The largest rejection of further study comes from the largest category, from which we may derive the reasonable inference that the most manifest rejection of something is often witnessed in the behaviour of

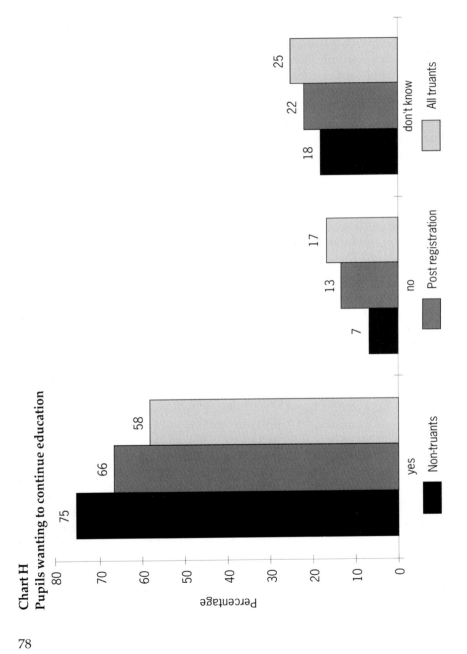

Chart H
Pupils wanting to continue education

those who most withdraw from it. But in this category more than a quarter have not yet decided, with the likelihood that those who eventually stay on at school will top 60 per cent (if only an extra six per cent or so decide to remain in education).

We need to ask, however, how strongly this apparent long-run endorsement of school and education connects with the success schools have in the struggle against truancy. This is the subject matter of Table Thirty Four A.

Table Thirty Four A
Schools ranked by percentages of pupils who want to continue their education

	Mean truancy level %
Twenty five schools with largest percentage of pupils wanting to continue education	26.1
Middle 100 schools	31.0
Twenty five schools with smallest percentage of pupils wanting to continue education	36.0

The effect here is very sizeable. The one internalised control on truancy we have uncovered which does seem to exert a marked effect, is this intention to continue education. Why it should differ so drastically from the other approbatory measures we considered is not clear. If finding school enjoyable or not, or useful or not, makes little difference, why should variations in the stated intention to stay on exert an effect on truancy levels?

It is possible that large numbers of would-be stayers on intend to move to FE college. For such respondents a positive endorsement of education, rather than school, may be signalled. In any case, the course team find this result mysterious in terms of the slight effect recorded in connection with other 'internalised' controls. Indisputably, overall, minatory controls seem to have a greater effect on preventing children from truanting than does the influence of various positive evaluations of school. This does not mean that these internalised forms of approval are not important in the attendance of most pupils. Without them, the already high incidence of truancy would be higher still. By no means can the conclusion be drawn that only greater vigilance matters in the battle against truancy. The evidence seems to be that schools could improve attendance levels where these are depressed by high levels of truancy:

(i)   By tightening up on controls.
(ii) By promoting an ethos where education is valued.
(iii) By improving those parts of the curriculum which seem to be subject to particularly high levels of truancy.

Finally, we should note that the answers given to questions such as whether school was enjoyable, and if the pupils were likely to stay on, may fluctuate. They may vary both with the *year* in which they are asked and the particular *time* of the year when the question is posed. It is important to mention this because, as we shall see, we have some evidence that the levels of truancy recorded in the half term on which we based our survey, are lower than those in longer periods, e.g. one year.

Truancy in the previous academic year

One obviously interesting question is whether truancy is fluid or rather static. The research team believes that although its investigations are cross-sectional, there are good grounds for thinking that the cross-sectional picture of a truancy level considerably higher for Year 11 than for Year 10 suggests very strongly that this will be apparent year after year as pupils pass from Year 10 to Year 11. One way into the problem is to ask respondents what happened last year.

Since the question of the genesis of truancy is one of general social-scientific as well as educational interest, it was always indicated that we should ask all pupils whether they truanted in the previous year. Inevitably, in the case of Year 10 pupils, this gave us some insight into Year 9 behaviour, though strictly speaking it was not part of our brief to investigate 14 year olds. In some respects, however, the results are fascinating. The first set appear in Table Thirty Five below. In this table Years 10 and 11 are not differentiated. It is noteworthy that 42 per cent of all pupils truanted either in the half term of the survey or in the previous year. This result is the sum of:

1. All this year's truants who truanted last year (20 per cent)
2. All this year's truants who did not truant last year (10 per cent)
3. All this year's non-truants who truanted last year (12 per cent).

This 42 per cent is higher than the mean level of truancy for the sample as a whole (30.5 per cent). It is also higher than the mean for Year 11 of 36 per cent.

Table Thirty Five
Pupils who say they truanted in the previous year

Base: all pupils

	Truanted previous year %	Did not truant previous year %
Truants	20	10
Non-Truants	12	58
Total	32	68

Tables Thirty Six and Thirty Seven break this data down into Years 10 and 11.

Table Thirty Six
Year 11 pupils saying they truanted in the previous year

Base: all Year 11 pupils

	Truanted previous year %	Did not truant previous year %
Truants	25	11
Non-truants	13	51
Total	38	62

Table Thirty Seven
Year 10 pupils saying they traunted in the previous year

Base: all Year 10 pupils

	Truanted previous year %	Did not truant previous year %
Truants	16	9
Non-truants	11	64
Total	27	73

Some readers might look at Table Thirty Six and conclude that the level of truancy given for the last year (38 per cent) is close to the level in the current Year 11 during our researched half term (36 per cent). They might also allege that in Table Thirty Seven the present Year 10 say that 27 per cent of them truanted in Year 9, again near to the mean percentage of

10 pupils in our half term of 25 per cent. Are we, then, looking at two stable cohorts with relatively unchanging habits of attendance and truancy? Such a contention would overturn the claim made much of earlier in this report, to the effect that truancy seems to increase very markedly between Years 10 and 11.

This alternative hypothesis, however, is not plausible. We see in Tables Thirty Five, Thirty Six and Thirty Seven that some pupils who truanted last year have not truanted this year and vice-versa, indeed that sizeable percentages of pupils change in this way. It is true that in Table Thirty Six we find that across the whole of Year 10 last year there was, according to present Year 11 pupils, a level of 38 per cent of pupils who truanted at some time. This is much higher than the level for Year 10 in the current survey. This does not mean that last Year's Year 10 were more notable truants than this year's. It means only that we are comparing truancy over three terms with that over a half term. Alongside the other underestimations built into this research, we now place another. The half term time-base is not a good guide to the whole year. Over longer periods higher rates are detectable.

The case is strong that truancy is fluid and also that it grows between the two years. Table Thirty Six shows that, of present Year 11 pupils, the number who at some time have truanted either in this present half term or in the previous year, is 49 per cent. That is, during a period of some eighteen months, almost half the present Year 11 pupils surveyed engaged in some kind of truancy. Earlier work on BT and PRT by two of the course team suggested that pupils say they have been engaging in much more truancy over long periods than the pupils in the present research say they have been involved in during the much shorter research period. This earlier research, undertaken in the Easter term with Year 11 (5) pupils, asking them to say if any had truanted at any time since the start of their GCSE courses, produced figures of up to 70 per cent.[1]

Fluidity is also witnessed in the way some schools buck the trend of apparently higher truancy levels in Year 11 than in Year 10. The present research shows that some schools have higher truancy in their Year 10 than in Year 11. In Chapter Three (page 40) we saw that in the present sample of schools there were twenty eight in which the level of truancy was higher in

Year 10 than in Year 11. The picture suggests considerable fluidity, with pupils switching into and out of the activity. We may also conjecture that truancy levels rise in the summer term – which is not our concern at the moment. Such a result would be reasonable, but the matter awaits research.

Table Thirty Seven suggests a level of truancy of 27 per cent during the course of Year 9 – somewhat higher than the level recorded in the survey half term of 25 per cent for the present Year 10. All these three tables suggest higher truancy levels over a whole year than in the particular half term under direct scrutiny. Perhaps across a whole year we should expect to add to the levels we found in our half term, an extra incidence of very infrequent truancy, i.e. taking place less than once per half term. Alternatively, perhaps the summer term has a higher level of truancy than the other two terms.

Finally it has to be admitted that, in the absence of time series study, we cannot definitely establish that there are systematic differences between the successive years of schooling which make truancy fluctuate, nor that it fluctuates upwards. Our results do show, however, that some children truanting in our half term did not do so in the last year, and some not truanting in our half term did so the previous year. Reflection and observation suggest that between years there are marked, systematic differences in the school experience, so that being in year 9 is a different experience from being in Year 10, and Year 10 different from Year 11, and that these experiences produce different truancy patterns.

In this case one hypothesis might be that truancy levels drop between Years 9 and 10 with the initial pull of examination programmes, and then rise again as disenchantment sets in. Until further research is done we shall not learn the likely answers to these questions. But it seems implausible that the experience of different years should be associated with globally static levels of truancy, so that Year 11's registering higher truancy than Year 10 in the current research does not indicate a change between years 10 and 11 which is likely to repeat itself, but rather the existence of two adjacent cohorts with fixed differences in their propensity to truant. After all, to pursue the objection to absurdity, could it be posited that these Year 11 children came in at Year 7 already disposed to truant in some way or other at a level of 36 per cent each half term?

Our data show that truancy levels were higher in Year 11 than in Year 10 during the half term under research. Other evidence from our survey, though less secure factually, combines with reflection on the different pressures operating in successive school years, to suggest that levels do rise between Years 10 and 11.

References
1. Stoll, P. and O'Keeffe, D. J. *Officially Present: An Investigation into Post Registration Truancy in Nine Maintained Schools* Institute of Economic Affairs Education Unit, 1989.

6 Truancy: The socio-economic and institutional context

Levels of truancy are affected by the socio-economic environment of schools. They are also influenced by institutional and managerial variations in school administration, which do not touch directly on questions of the popularity or otherwise of subjects and teachers. Such effects are not surprising. Nor do they in any sense run counter to the hypothesis that truancy is more than anything else a curricular phenomenon, a response to aspects of the lessons on offer, which are seen, for a variety of reasons, as unsatisfactory and unrewarding. Many children in the poorer regions of the country, or from low income groups in affluent areas, may find, quite simply, that the margin of choice between the curriculum as a desirable good, and non-attendance, comes at a lower threshold than is the case with their better off peers. There may be pressures to look after siblings, ailing parents and so on. What seems likely, from the evidence of our survey, though it remains strictly speaking not demonstrable, is that the 'poverty factor' connects more with high absence levels from school, and thus with implicitly high levels of BT, than with directly measurable levels of truancy manifestly much higher than those elsewhere.

Regional variations

No significant regional variations emerged from these results. There might have been some finer meshed grid than the simple one we used – North/Midlands/South – but it is not obvious what that might have been. One favourable consideration attends this result. It does suggest in its consistency a parallel attention to consistency in the administration of the survey. Though no regional variation was recorded, there is some evidence, though less than might be expected, of an 'inner city' effect, and as we shall see later, of rather unpredictable, not to say surprising, variations between LEAs.

Inner city schools and others

There is some effect here on directly measurable truancy, but it is by no means very large. Schools categorised (in the heads' questionnaires) as mainly inner city, or inner city and industrial, have a mean truancy level of 32.9 per cent against 30.5 per cent for all others. For mainly suburban or prosperous suburban schools the figure is 30.1 per cent and for prosperous suburban only, the figure is 28.5 per cent. These are significant but rather slight differences.

When we consider the evidence given by headteachers, we find that the correlation between their estimated percentages of inner city pupils and truancy levels is 0.14 – barely significant. Interestingly, if we correlate this variable against absence levels (the percentage of pupils absent on the day of the [pupil] questionnaires) we get a figure of 0.55. This can account for 30 per cent of the variance.

Absence and the inner city school

In the schools were heads maintained that no pupils were of inner city background, the mean absence level was 13.6 per cent. In schools where 50 per cent or more pupils were from the inner city areas, the mean absence level was 26.3 per cent. This is consistent with the view that inner city schools have higher levels of truancy than other schools, but also that this mainly takes the form of BT and is thus difficult to establish positively. It also supports our earlier contention that truancy levels are higher than measured in the survey, particularly for schools with high absence rates.

Table Thirty Eight
Absence levels and the socio-economic composition of schools

Base: all schools

	Mean absence levels %
Schools which heads say have no inner city pupils	13.6
Schools which heads say have 50% or more inner city pupils	26.3

This is a very large effect, but it does not demonstrate directly a higher level of truancy. There will also be justified absence. Our earlier discussion suggests that this absence level will contain considerable unrecorded BT.

Free school meals

There is a small but significant effect on truancy here. In schools with a low proportion of free school meals, the mean truancy level is 28.5 per cent compared to the sample mean of 31 per cent. In schools with a high percentage of free school meals the level rises to 34.1 per cent. Pupils in schools with a high proportion of such meals do truant more than those in schools with lower proportions, though it is important to note that we have no direct evidence that it is the recipients of free meals who truant. The difference seems comparable in size to the small advantage in terms of non-truanting enjoyed by non-county schools over county schools, or single sex girls' schools over mixed schools (see below). Nor, especially in a period when unemployment has increased very rapidly, should we take free school meals as a good proxy for the inner city syndrome or even for the effects of poverty as such.

The correlation of free school meals with truancy levels is in any case rather weak (0.17). This cannot account for more than 2 per cent of the variance. Interestingly, the correlation of free meals with attendance levels again yields a much stronger result (0.65). This could account for 42 per cent of the variance. As with inner city effects, with which free school meals cannot be by any means equated, this evidence points implicitly to higher levels of persistent BT in such schools. Whatever 'poverty' free school meals may indicate, however, it cannot be taken as more than a partial explanation of such absence.

The twenty five schools with the smallest percentage of pupils entitled to free school meals have mean truancy and absence levels of 28.5 per cent and 9.9 per cent respectively. This compares to overall means of truancy and attendance levels of 31 per cent and 17.3 per cent. The corresponding statistics for the twenty five schools with the highest numbers entitled to free school meals are 34.4 per cent and 27.7 per cent. These results are displayed in Table Thirty Nine.

These are significant but not very large differences in truancy levels, comparable to the inner city effects noted above. There is almost a 6 per cent difference between truancy levels in the schools with the least and the most free meals. But the spread is not great; neither extreme is far from the mean. It is the differences in *attendance* levels which are most dramatic. Here the yawning gap between the most and the least favoured schools,

Table Thirty Nine
Truancy, school absence and free school meals

Base: all schools

	Truancy level %	Absence level %
Twenty five schools with highest nos. of free school meals	34.4	27.7
Twenty five schools with lowest nos. of free school meals	28.5	9.9
Overall	31.0	17.3

suggests a hidden and, we repeat, strictly unprovable (within our present research constraints) BT of considerable magnitude.

Pupil–teacher ratios and truancy

One very interesting result, small but significant, runs rather against the popular wisdom. As pupil–teacher ratios decline, so truancy levels increase slightly. Too much cannot be read into this result, but it is interesting that the two variables move conversely. At the very least, the repeated claims for the benefits supposedly derived from schools having more teachers, are not upheld in this one respect – they do not generate better attendance. It is true that the truancy levels in schools with more teachers might be worse if they did not have those teachers, but this is mere counterfactual speculation. The evidence from this survey points the opposite way. Admittedly, lower pupil–teacher ratios should not be associated mechanically with smaller classes. Pupil–teacher ratios may be better considered as a resource variable, with lower ratios mostly a function of more funds spent on support teachers and teachers with lighter timetables. The evidence, such as it is, is that whatever is done with the extra teachers, the result is *not* lower levels of measurable truancy.

Table Forty
Pupil–teacher ratios and truancy

Pupil–teacher ratio	Average truancy level %
<14.5	32.5
14.5 to 16.5	31.4
>16.5	29.2

If on the other hand we correlate truancy levels with pupil–teacher ratios, the correlation is –0.14, a similar effect to that in the case of free school meals.

Truancy differences between boys and girls

There is no marked difference between the truancy of boys and girls overall. The rates are 31 per cent for boys and 30 per cent for girls. The slightly lower rate for girls is mainly due to the influence of the data obtained from single sex schools for girls. The separate data for Years 10 and 11 yield a very different picture. While truancy climbs considerably between the two years, the growth in male truancy is a lot more marked. (See Table Forty One)

Table Forty One
Percentage of boys and girls truanting from school

Base: all pupils

	Yes %	No %	Total %
Boys Year 10	24.6	75.4	100
Girls Year 10	25.5	74.5	100
Boys Year 11	37.7	62.3	100
Girls Year 11	30.5	69.5	100

Even when we duly observe the very remarkable climb in boys' truancy between Years 10 and 11, compared to a much more modest, though still considerable, increase in the numbers of girls who truant, we are still far from endorsing the old notion that truancy is predominantly a male phenomenon. This is simply not borne out by these results. This may have implications for the extension of the traditional connection between boys and truancy into the further notion that truancy and juvenile deliquency are cognate phenomena. (See Chapter Two, especially Reid and Metcalfe[1]) Juvenile deliquency is undoubtedly predominantly male in character. But if truancy is not especially male-dominated, while juvenile crime is, the notion of a causal nexus between truancy and delinquency needs to be treated rather cautiously.

Single sex versus mixed schools

Interestingly, the picture here is rather different. Single sex girls' schools have consistently lower levels of truancy than either mixed or single sex boys' schools. Levels at single sex boys' schools are higher than at mixed schools. There are too few single sex boys' schools in our sample, however, to admit of any inference. There were eighteen single sex girls' schools, which does permit reasonable confidence in the result. Any such effect clearly belongs in the bracket 'institutional difference' and is mildly conceivable as a result of the difference in ethos between these schools. If there is a distinctive ethos in these girls' schools it could in principle relate either to their being girls' schools or to their being selective schools, or both. These different results, robust or weak, are presented in Table Forty Two.

The result for single sex schools overall is, as has been explained, misleading, because of the paucity of boys-only schools. Nevertheless, there is clear implicit evidence that something favourable happens to girls' perception of schools when they are taught together. Conversely, there is some apparent diminution in the force of ethos when boys are admitted to the same institution as girls. Finally, there is a weak suggestion that the same process *improves* the situation for boys. It is very hard to imagine what all this means if it does not mean variations in ethos caused by the presence or absence of single sex education. It also suggests a divergence of interests between parents of boys and girls, with the former gaining and the latter losing by co-education.

Table Forty Two
Truancy levels (percentages) in single sex and mixed schools

	Boys %	Girls %	All %
Mixed	31.7	31.2	31.6
Single sex (boys)	32.4		32.4
Single sex (girls)		26.4	26.4
Single sex (overall)			28.2

County schools compared with others

County schools have an average truancy level of 31.9 per cent compared to 28.8 per cent for other types. This is a small but significant difference which is certainly worth noting. It is about the same magnitude as the influence of free school meals taken as a 'poverty indicator', and is clear evidence that institutional factors affect attendance/truancy levels. This 'superior' performance of the non-county schools may afford us a glimpse of the 'ethos' factor at work. We cannot be sure that such an ethos is of the deliberately school-constructed kind which counteracts the background circumstances. It may simply be a mechanical reflection of background influences, such as those, for example, which may be channelled into school by selection. In any case in this instance any putative influence is small, as is apparent in Table Forty Three.

Table Forty Three
Percentage of truants in county schools and others

	Yes %	No %	Total %
County schools	31.9	68.1	100
Other	28.8	71.2	100

This is a real but not large effect. If it results from a school ethos deliberately maintained to counter adverse conditions, rather than being merely a background effect neutrally mediated by school, such ethos presumably registers itself both in extra care over subjects and teaching and in extra vigilance with regard to controls on attendance. We do not know.

The age-range and size of school

These have no apparent effect on levels of truancy. This finding was one which certainly surprised the Project Director, who has long believed that smaller schools can develop more effectively an academic and behavioural ethos and a supportive and convivial atmosphere than is the case with larger schools. Perhaps this belief should be consigned to the set of discarded shibboleths.

Attendance variations show up better than truancy variations

It has to be said that none of the socio-economic variations we have considered appears to effect large changes in truancy levels one way or the other. What we would expect – that low income groups do worse – does seem partly borne out. None of our socio-economic measures is much good, however, and large effects cannot be read off from small variations. Nor should one read for 'free school meals' either 'long-term poverty' or 'inner city' status. That said, it is also the case that some of the apparent effects of our socio-economic factors on attendance (rather than directly on truancy) were much more marked. This, by conjecture, we may take to be evidence that 'poorer' areas are characterised by higher levels of unmeasured BT. How much, we cannot know as yet.

With regard to institutional factors such as single sex education or otherwise, or county and non-county status, there did appear to be some modest effect, presumably mediated by differential ethos. It is impossible to know whether such ethos is a countervailing force or merely reflective of various background differentiations. In any event, nothing uncovered in this chapter constitutes very powerful evidence for the ethos thesis. We had hoped that heads' comments on their schools would yield a decent and decipherable picture of ethos variations. Alas, they tended to converge in repetitive affirmations of virtue. Before we consider throwing out the idea of ethos, however, let us consider finally what, if anything, our results from the pupils' responses do allow us to say on the question of ethos. This will be the subject matter of our last chapter.

References
1. Reid, K. and Kendall, L. 'A Review of Some Recent Research in Persistent School Absenteeism' *British Journal of Educational Studies* Volume 30 Part 3 (October, 1982)

7 A question of ethos

We have noted earlier that, as with much social science vocabulary, the language of educational theory and research is characterised by shifting and stipulative definitions. We have already made some reference in this report to the idea of 'ethos'. This, however, is a peculiarly elusive and difficult concept of the stipulative kind. While, for example, the word 'curriculum' has required a less ambiguous meaning of late, the notion of 'ethos' remains uncertain. Common sense would regard it as crucial, but what exactly is it, and what might its dimensions be?

Ethos

This ancient word is typically thought of as signifying the characteristic spirit, or prevalent tone of sentiment, of an institution or system. Some American research, such as Jencks[1] and Coleman[2], has implicitly ruled out much role for ethos, because social class is seen as overwhelming all other influences in determining educational performance. In fact the idea of background as the most important determinant of performance must not be confused with that of background as determining everything. What, if anything, is overwhelmed is the aggregate result, not the performance of specific individuals. If it were true that background ability and 'culture' determine all, and that school is a mere passive conduit for these inexorable forces, then ethos would be a non-starter, except for the logical truism that one set of pupils' backgrounds will produce one ethos in schools and another set a different one. Such fatalism ignores the reality of historical change, the emergence of an increasingly middle class population. Since this phenomenon must be mediated largely through education, it is the minority in any cross-sectional study whose performance is *not* predicted by the background determinants who matter; a minority whose constant move away from its origins produces in time an increasingly middle class formation, and a smaller working class base.

It is here that a concept like ethos comes into its own. It may be proposed that school ethos is a crucial factor in upward social mobility.

Something about the mental life of some schools interacts with the potential of their pupils in order to render some of them upwardly mobile. The still unanswered question is: what? The reason we need to know more about it is that it would be of great benefit in the general battle for standards. Authors such as Rutter have stressed the importance of school organisation,[3] and Cox and Marks[4] have shown the wide variations in examination attainment among schools of similar socio-economic location and profile. These latter findings uphold the likelihood that schools do possess different moral and intellectual atmospheres which are not mere functions of the backgrounds of their pupils, and that they do differentially encourage or inhibit academic performance, institutional identity, attendance and truancy, upward mobility and so on.

A reasonable hypothesis might be that a good school, i.e. one with an effective ethos, will generate high attendance, both encouraging and rewarding good attendance and work and applying sanctions to bad attendance and work. Such an ethos will suffuse the school's managerial policies. It will combine intellectual/moral agreements among the members of the school, and minatory controls to prevent and punish infractions of the school's rules and to combat would-be subversion of its purposes. This ethos may be continuous with home and other background influences, or discontinuous with them. As ethos affects truancy, it will control it both by making children want to come to school and lessons, and by being vigilant against the possibility that they may not; also by punishing them in the event that they deliberately do not. Prudent management will also seek, as it tries to prevent infractions, to understand their causes.

Changes in ethos could have dramatic results. Obviously in affluent circumstances school can easily confirm the home situation. It is more of a problem in difficult socio-economic circumstances, where the challenge facing a school is to turn dislike of school or lessons or indifference to them, into approbation or at least acceptance by a large minority of children.

The school/background interface

The problem with ethos is that it is easier to explore conceptually and even theoretically than it is to measure. The exact balance of influences on the behaviour of pupils of school age, that behaviour including attendance and truancy, is impossible to ascertain. Real events, however, – learning-success and learning-failure, attendance or truancy – must have causes. In the nature of things, it was not possible in our research to glean much about the individual backgrounds of children from their completed questionnaires, though we were able, via our headteacher questionnaires, to build up a limited social picture of the schools themselves. This latter did not mean, unfortunately, that we were able to construct even the most shadowy outline of an ethos pattern. Instead, some help came from another quarter. The oblique light thrown on the ethos question by children's responses to their questionnaires was much more revealing than anything the heads' questionnaires were able to give us. We have already made some discursive reference to school and parental deterrents on truancy in Chapter Five. As will be apparent in Tables Forty Four and Forty Five, there is much more deterrence brought to bear on the truancy phenomenon than there is condonation, both by parents and teachers. In this final chapter we attempt the difficult task of saying something a little more systematic about ethos.

The work on schools revealed, as we saw in the last chapter, a few positive correlations between inner city location, numbers of free school meals and truancy levels. The observable correlations between these independent variables and absence levels were stronger than correlations between the same variables and truancy levels. This probably does mean higher than measured BT, compounding the difficulties of measuring truancy *tout court*. These difficulties themselves we have noted repeatedly in earlier chapters. Within our resources and methodology they are accessible only to conjecture.

It was also apparent that slight effects on truancy seem to be exerted by institutional variations such as those between all girls, mixed, and all boys schools, and the differences, unexamined, between county and non-county status. It would be strange if these results did not in some degree indicate variations in ethos, but quite simply, we have no way of tracking them.

It should be remembered that, while we have come at the problem of truancy via two levels of aggregation – the numbers of individual respondents (37,451) and the numbers of schools (150) – there is a third: our twenty randomly selected LEAs. Strangely, a surface scanning of overall performance of the LEAs in our sample does not confirm what we may term 'conventional' expectations. For example, very depressed areas in the North of England might be expected to manifest much higher than average levels of measured truancy. Among our twenty LEAs this sort of pattern proved quite simply not to be the case. Maybe if we could get at the 'missing' data on BT the picture would be different. We cannot, however, and contemplation of the information we do possess leads to the strong suspicion that ethos is indeed intimately involved in the results. While the aggregate data do reveal, as we have seen, a small but positive inner city and socio-economic effect (the latter measured in relation to the proportion of free school meals) when we looked at the differential performance by our twenty LEAs (whose identities we cannot for ethical and contractual reasons reveal), the most striking thing was that the 'poverty factor' was not visible: quite the contrary in fact. For this reason we reproduce a performance table, with the names of the LEAs removed and with only the vaguest of geographical identities.

Table Forty Four
Performance of LEAs from lowest levels of truancy to highest
Base: all schools

		%	No. of schools
1.	Northern	25.3	7
2.	Northern	25.4	4
3.	London	26.5	3
4.	Midland	27.7	4
5.	Southern	28.0	10
6.	Northern	28.2	4
7.	Northern	28.6	5
8.	Northern	29.6	3
9.	London	29.7	4
10.	Southern	30.6	8
10.	Southern	30.6	17
12.	Midland	31.2	20
13.	London	32.2	4
14.	Southern	32.6	25
15.	Northern	33.4	4
16.	Southern	33.8	7
16.	Northern	33.8	3
16.	Northern	33.8	10
19.	London	34.2	3
20.	Midland	38.8	5

A number of caveats is needed. First, we could not provide convincing socio-economic indicators for these LEAs, and have resorted instead to crude geographical markers. This limits the explanatory value of our rank order. Moreover, the numbers of schools in the authorities vary considerably, though readers will remember that, advisedly, we took 25 per cent of the schools in each LEA selected. We have not tried to sort out inter LEA variations by type of truancy, such as BT, PRT and mixtures thereof. Nor have we sought to see if there is much difference between LEAs on Year by Year variations or in the propensities of boys or girls to truant. Then there are the considerations treated at length in earlier chapters: above all, the main category 'truanted at least once in the last half term' is not a sensitive one. It may conceal very different hard core patterns.

Even so we were startled to find the lowest levels of truancy (on this rather blunt measure of 'truanted at least once in the last half term') associated with notoriously depressed areas. This is true of the first three LEAs in the rank order for example, and of the sixth, seventh and eighth. So startling was the discovery that a poor northern LEA apparently did best, on this crude measure, in the battle against truancy, and indeed contained the lowest scoring school of the whole 150, while many affluent areas had high levels of truancy in the schools we visited, that our thoughts turned inevitably to school organisation and ethos. At the very least it seems that whatever underlying background factors there may be behind truancy, schools and LEAs can in some degree overthrow them. If background were all, depressed areas should not be able to outperform prosperous ones in retaining the interests and presence of children. As it happens some of the LEAs recording high levels of truancy are in very favoured environments indeed.

Perhaps a comprehensively national survey of truancy would yield a different picture, one corresponding to what we have termed conventional assumptions. Perhaps, on the other hand, we are overstating the surprising character of our result. After all, we now know that there can be similar surprises in the academic performance of LEAs. This was clearly revealed in the academic league tables published in the autumn of 1992. Furthermore, the bucking of socio-economic trends is a recognised commonplace *within* LEAs, as writers as different as Rutter[5], and Cox and

Marks[6] have shown. Why, therefore, should there not be such reversals of expectation – in forms like low levels of measurable truancy – in comparisons made *between* LEAs? There certainly are in our twenty chosen authorities. All caveats issued, the question is not whether, but why or how, this can be so. There must be something different about how the schools we visited in these LEAs treat their children. But what? We repeat: the notions 'ethos' and 'organisation' come inevitably to mind.

Given that the data from heads and the people they delegated to fill in questionnaires yielded little on the question of ethos, what can we derive from looking at the pupil data? As we have said, here the situation, while not excellent, is nevertheless much better.

School organisation and ethos

It is extremely difficult to give any quantitative interpretation of school ethos, but the data are at least consistent with the contention that it is of central importance. In Table Forty Five it should be noted that the numbers of non-truants are twice as great as those of truants. Very much more truancy is deterred by parents and teachers than is condoned by them. It is true that in aggregate data such as these, schools could in principle be taken as passively mediating the influence of background. In such a case 'ethos' would be a mere mechanistic name for the continuity between home and school. But as we saw in Table Forty Four, this seems simply not to be the case. Schools and LEAs can and do 'interrupt' the process of social reproduction. Among the majority of approximately 25,000 pupils in our survey who are non-truants, very many must be deterred by teacher vigilance or home solidarity with school, against the thrust of socio-economic 'background'. In Table Forty Five success against truancy shows up much more markedly than failure.

Table Forty Five
Successful and unsuccessful school and parental controls on truancy

(1) Successful
Base: all non-truants

		%
(i)	Non-truants deterred by parents	48
(ii)	Non-truants deterred by teachers	38

(2) Unsuccessful
Base: all truants

(iii)	Truants saying parents know	44
(iv)	Truants saying parents do not know	36
(v)	Truants saying they do not know if parents know	13
(vi)	Truants saying teachers know	30
(vii)	Truants saying teachers do not know	38
(viii)	Truants not knowing if teachers know	25

NB It is important to remember the difference in the sizes of the two bases here, non-truants outnumbering truants by two to one. The picture is mixed, but encouraging overall. Some gloomy reflection can be extracted. While (iii) and (vi) are worrying from the point of view of school and family slackness/firmness, (iv), (v), (vii) and (viii) seem scarcely better in the same regard. Teachers and parents for the most part should know if children truant, and children should know whether parents and teachers know.

In fact, there is much more comfort than gloom in this table. Almost half of potential truants are put off by the thought of parental disapproval. The same applies to more than a third of potential truants in relation to their teachers. Many of these two groups will overlap, in what can justifiably be seen as a successful stand against truancy by parents and teachers; home and school in concert. Most important, Table Forty Four suggests that much of this stand takes place against the trend of socio-economic prediction. Even if this alleged fear of parental or teacher anger is not entirely accurate, one may reasonably infer that in the absence of parental and teacher vigilance there would be truly massive increases in truancy.

By far the largest deterrents to truancy are parental and teacher disapproval. Minatory controls such as these, however, have no implications *vis à vis* the positive internalisation of putative school ethos on the part of pupils. They may believe partly that truancy is wrong. All we know is that many of them say they would truant but for fear of parental and teacher displeasure. On the other hand, in terms of the teacher/parent link these results may well give evidence of shared ethos. Greater teacher vigilance and closer school/home liaison might expand considerably on the figure of two thirds of pupils who do not truant. Take the case of truants whose parents do not know. They are a category in limbo, suspended between those whose parents do know and would-be truants deterred by the prospect of parents knowing. They have this status because it is reasonable to assume a fair proportion of them would be prevented if parental knowledge were probable. Similar considerations apply to those truants who say their teachers do not know.

As we saw in Chapter Five school vigilance matters enormously. Let us look again at Table Twenty Nine.

Table Twenty Nine (also on p. 68)
Truancy levels of schools ranked by ease of truancy

	Truancy level %
Twenty five schools with largest percentage of truants finding truancy easy	33.7
Middle 100 schools	31.6
Twenty five schools with smallest percentages of truants finding truancy easy	26.0

It is quite evident here that school vigilance, probably often in conjunction with parental backup – the question did not ask what made truancy difficult or easy, merely which it was – can make a considerable difference.

The perceived usefulness of lessons also provides a correlation of −0.22 with truancy levels. This can explain 4 per cent of the variance, which is less than we expected. The correlation for perceived enjoyment of school and truancy levels is even smaller (−0.18). There is a real effect in these cases, but it is small. Positive endorsement of the curriculum does not seem to generate much holding force. This is probably because of the high correlation between truancy and ease of truancy. Large numbers of pupils who, broadly speaking, accept the curricular fare on offer, nevertheless do not esteem it to the degree required for them not to truant if they have the chance.

We are back again to minatory controls. All social order relies on a mixture of such controls and internalised rules. Our human clay is probably as weak in school as elsewhere. The mixture of encouragement and command which should be used must always be problematic. There is a limit, especially within the traditions of a free society, to what force we may apply to meet generally agreed social purposes. We must accept that there are limits also to the extent to which we can expect pupils positively to applaud what comes their way as compulsory public knowledge. For example, if we push them too hard in the case of PRT the level of BT may go up, and vice-versa. Such reflection brings us up against the whole question of the huge intrusion into adolescent life caused by compulsory education. This cannot be pursued far here save to say that, if some of their lessons are of low quality, then some secondary pupils will truant on the basis of rational calculation. Who can blame them, or expect anything else? A free society lacks the coercive mechanisms whereby educational material, about which a large minority has reservations, can be totally enforced.

It may be – on reflection – that we have not been sufficiently sensitive in our measurement of the pupils' enjoyment of school and reckoning of the value of subject-matter. It is worth looking again at Table Twenty Five in this regard.

Table Twenty Five (also on p. 64)
Reasons for not truanting

Base: all non-truants

		%
Parents. Concern that parents would find out	(Pa)	48
Not miss school (do not want to)	(M)	40
School. Concern that school might find out	(S)	38
Pointless to truant	(Po)	10
Miss work (did not want to)	(W)	6
Education is important	(E)	6
Like school	(L)	3

Many pupils say that they do not want to miss their lessons. This does suggest, at the least, a utilitarian concern with their own learning. If we are more optimistic, it may also reflect a positive, if partial internalisa-tion of the purposes of school on the part of non-truants. Reconsideration of Table Twenty Five shows that many non-truants seem rather positive about school. Forty per cent say they do not want to miss school. Ten per cent regard truancy as pointless. This conviction is rather amorphous, but is at least consistent with acceptance of school, though wide differences ranging from passive to active acceptance are probably indicated. Six per cent say they do not want to miss the work, a consideration that could span prudential care, utilitarian advantage or conviction that the work is interesting and important in its own right. A further 6 per cent simply say that education is important. A small group (3 per cent) go as far as to say they do not truant because they like school.

By far the best measure of ethos we do have *is* one relating to internalised approval. This is the relatively high correlation between the percentage of pupils intending to continue their education and truancy levels. This statistic is −0.36, which can account for 13 per cent of the variance. To the possible objection that prudential behaviour in relation to the school/work link is not to be regarded as internalised approval, we may reply that on the contrary it is consistent with it and often may be a constitutive part of it.

Whatever the precise and variable components of ethos, it is already clear that ethos factors are both consensual and minatory. Like other forms of social control, the controls placed on children are a mixture. It is also apparent that there is much which schools can do to control and reduce levels of truancy. Some schools and some LEAs evidently do much to suppress the propensity to truant exists among their pupils while others do much less. Whether such suppression takes the form of merely containing truancy through external controls, or of persuading children to accept freely the purposes of school and lessons, or both, is a topic needing further research. However, we have uncovered some evidence that, for the present, minatory disincentives to truancy remain paramount.

What we might have looked at and missed: school atmosphere

It should be noted, finally, though this is to enter a realm of conjecture beyond our evidence base, that there is more to the popularity of school than positive estimations of the value of lessons. There is also the question of the social attractions of school. It may be useful to propose that schools have an overall atmosphere comprising both their ethos and their social conviviality. A strong academic ethos will pull children into curricular conformity or consensus. A feeling of conviviality will lead to schools being attractive in the sense of being a youth club. Sadly, we did not investigate this possibility, though questions designed to elicit information about its force could easily be built into subsequent work. The hypothesis which could guide such a research initiative is simply put: schools with very low levels of truancy will score very high, both on ethos and on conviviality.

References

1. Jencks, C. S. *et al Inequality: A Reassessment of the Effect of Family and Schooling in America* Basic Books, 1972

2. Coleman, J. S. *et al Equality of Educational Opportunity* National Centre for Educational Statistics, 1966

3. Rutter, M. *et al Fifteen Thousand Hours* Open Books, 1979

4. Their work with Maciej Pomian-Srzednicki is typical of their ongoing work. See Cox, C., Marks J. and Pomian-Szrednicki, M. *Standards in English Schools* NCES, 1983

5. Rutter *op cit.*

6. Cox *et al op cit.*

Appendix A

Pupil Questionnaire

We would like to find out your opinions about your lessons and school, and discover if you truanted (did not come to school when you were supposed to), or registered and left school, or skipped lessons in the last half term. You should *not* write your name on the questionnaire. None of your teachers will know what you have written. It will be completely confidential.

	DAY	MONTH	YEAR	
TODAY'S DATE				(10–15)

School Year

TICK ONE BOX ONLY

Year 10 (4) ☐ 1 (16)

Year 11 (5) ☐ 2

TICK ONE BOX ONLY

Female ☐ 1 (17)

Male ☐ 2

Q1.   In the last half term have you ever stayed away from school when you were not supposed to, or registered and then left school, or skipped lessons?

TICK ONE BOX ONLY

Yes ☐ 1 (18)

No ☐ 2

IF YOUR ANSWER IS 'NO' PLEASE GO TO QUESTION 10.

Q2a.   In the last half term how often have you skipped lessons?

TICK ONE BOX ONLY

Every day ☐ 1 (19)

2–4 times a week ☐ 2

Once a week ☐ 3

2–3 times a month ☐ 4

Once a month ☐ 5

Less often ☐ 6

Never ☐ 7

IF YOUR ANSWER IS 'NEVER' PLEASE GO TO QUESTION 3a.

Q2b. In the last half term did you skip options more or less than you skipped other subjects?

TICK ONE BOX ONLY

More [ ] 1 (20)

No difference [ ] 2

Less [ ] 3

Q3a. In the last half term how often have you registered and then left school?

TICK ONE BOX ONLY

Every day [ ] 1 (21)

2–4 times a week [ ] 2

Once a week [ ] 3

2–3 times a month [ ] 4

Once a month [ ] 5

Less often [ ] 6

Never [ ] 7

IF YOUR ANSWER IS 'NEVER' PLEASE GO TO QUESTION 4a.

Q3b. In the last half term what is the largest number of days when you have been absent from school at any one time when you registered and then left school?

TICK ONE BOX ONLY

More than a week [ ] 1 (22)

A week [ ] 2

3–4 days [ ] 3

2 days [ ] 4

1 day [ ] 5

Less than a day [ ] 6

Q4a. In the last half term how often have you not come to school at all when you were supposed to?

TICK ONE BOX ONLY

Every day	☐	1 (23)
2–4 times a week	☐	2
Once a week	☐	3
2–3 times a month	☐	4
Once a month	☐	5
Less often	☐	6
Never	☐	7

IF YOUR ANSWER IS 'NEVER' PLEASE GO TO QUESTION 5a.

Q4b. What is the largest number of days you have stayed away from school when you were supposed to come, at any one time in the last half term?

TICK ONE BOX ONLY

More than a week	☐	1 (24)
A week	☐	2
3–4 days	☐	3
2 days	☐	4
1 day	☐	5
Less than a day	☐	6

Q5a. In the last half term have you ever not come to school when you were supposed to, or left school after registration because you did not like school?

TICK BOX FOR YES.   ☐ 1 (25)

IF YOUR ANSWER WAS YES, PLEASE WRITE A FEW WORDS EXPLAINING WHY YOU DO NOT LIKE SCHOOL.

_____   (26) (27) (28)

_____

_____

Q5b. In the last term have you ever not come to school when you
were supposed to, or left school after registration, or skipped
a lesson because you wanted to miss a particular lesson?

TICK BOX FOR YES. ☐ 1 (29)

IF YOUR ANSWER WAS YES, PLEASE LIST THE LESSONS AND
WRITE A FEW WORDS EXPLAINING WHY YOU WANTED TO
MISS EACH SUBJECT.

Subject   *Reason for missing lesson*

_____ _____ (30) (31) (32)

_____ _____

_____ _____

_____ _____

_____ _____

_____ _____

Q5c. In the last half term have you ever not come to school when
you were supposed to, or left school after registration, or skipped lessons for any other reason?

TICK BOX FOR YES. ☐ 1 (33)

IF YOUR ANSWER WAS YES, PLEASE WRITE A FEW WORDS
EXPLAINING YOUR REASON.

_____ (34) (35) (36)

_____

_____

Q6. Does either of your parents know that you did not go to school
when you were supposed to, or left school after registration, or
skipped lessons in the last half term?

TICK ONE BOX ONLY   Yes, one or both knows ☐ 1 (37)

No, neither knows ☐ 2

I don't know if either knows ☐ 3

108

Q7. Does any of your teachers know that you did not come to school when you were supposed to, or left school after registration, or skipped lessons in the last half term?

TICK ONE BOX ONLY

At least one teacher knows | 1 (38)

No teacher knows | 2

I don't know if any teacher knows | 3

Q8. If you left school after registration or skipped lessons in the last half term, how easy was it to avoid getting caught?

TICK ONE BOX ONLY

Easy | 1 (39)

Not particularly easy or difficult | 2

Difficult | 3

Q9. In the last half term if you left school after registration or skipped lessons, was this . . .?

TICK ONE BOX ONLY

Always alone | 1 (40)

Always with friends | 2

Sometimes alone and sometimes with friends | 3

Q10. In the last half term have any of your friends left school after registration or skipped lessons?

TICK ONE BOX ONLY

Yes | 1 (41)

No | 2

I do not know | 3

Q11. Did you ever leave school after registration or skip lessons last year?

TICK ONE BOX ONLY

Yes | 1 (42)

No | 2

STUDENTS WHO HAVE AT ANY TIME NOT COME TO SCHOOL WHEN THEY WERE SUPPOSED TO, OR LEFT SCHOOL AFTER REGISTRATION, OR SKIPPED LESSONS IN THE LAST HALF TERM SHOULD LEAVE OUT QUESTION 12.

Q12. If you did not leave school after registration or skip lessons in the last half term, was this because . . .?

TICK ONE BOX ONLY

Your parents might have found out ☐ 1 (43)

Your school might have found out ☐ 2

You did not want to miss school ☐ 3

Other reasons ☐ 4

PLEASE WRITE DOWN THESE REASONS.

_____ (44) (45) (46)

_____

_____

Q13. Do you think school is enjoyable or not?

TICK ONE BOX ONLY.

Always enjoyable ☐ 1 (47)

Mostly enjoyable ☐ 2

Neither enjoyable nor unenjoyable ☐ 3

Mostly not enjoyable ☐ 4

Never enjoyable ☐ 5

PLEASE WRITE DOWN A FEW WORDS EXPLAINING YOUR ANSWER.

_____ (48) (49) (50)

_____

_____

Q14. Do you think what you are learning now in school will be useful when you leave?
TICK ONE BOX ONLY.

Yes, all of it will be useful	☐	1 (51)
Most of it will be useful	☐	2
About half of it will be useful	☐	3
Only a small part will be useful	☐	4
None of it will be useful	☐	5

Q15. Please write down the names of the subjects you have been taking in the last half term.

_____ (52) (53) (54)

_____

_____

Q16. How many GCSE examinations do you expect to take?
PLEASE WRITE THE NUMBER IN THE BOX.

Number of GCSE subjects ☐ (55–56)

Q17. Would you like to continue with your education at school or college after you have finished the 11(5)th year?
TICK ONE BOX ONLY.

Yes	☐	1 (57)
No	☐	2
I don't know	☐	3

THANK YOU FOR HELPING US BY FILLING IN THIS QUESTIONNAIRE.

111

Appendix B

Post-Registration Truancy Research 1991–92
Questionnaire for Headteachers

Q1. **Roll of School Today**
Type of School (Grammar, Modern, Comprehensive, Technical). If your
School is some other type please specify:

_____ (10)

Status (County or Voluntary) _____ (11)

Age-range of School _____ (12)

	Boys		Girls	
Number of pupils in year 10 (4)	☐	(13–15)	☐	(16–18)
in year 11 (5)	☐	(19–21)	☐	(22–24)
Pupils on roll in whole school	☐	(25–28)	☐	(29–32)

Q2. **Free School Meals**
Number of pupils in the school **eligible** for free school meals ☐ (33–35)

113

Q3. **Assessment of Catchment Area**
NB This is an assessment of the environment the children come from, not of the location of the school.
1) Rural – farms, villages, small country and seaside towns.
2) Inner City and Overspill – decayed housing and high rise blocks, etc. Some new town high rise may qualify, especially as they repeat inner city problems in new settings.
3) Established manufacturing areas, with few highly favoured but very few disadvantaged pupils.
4) Prosperous suburban, with high owner occupancy.
5) Less prosperous suburban.
Please show the approximate percentage of pupils in years 10 (4) and 11 (5) who come from each catchment area:

Catchment Area

	1	2	3	4	5
Year 10 (4)	☐ %	☐ %	☐ %	☐ %	☐ %
	(36–38)	(39–41)	(42–44)	(45–47)	(48–50)
Year 11 (5)	☐ %	☐ %	☐ %	☐ %	☐ %
	(51–53)	(54–56)	(57–59)	(60–62)	(63–65)

Q4. **Mathematics Examination**
1) Expected Mathematics Examination Targets
Number of pupils expected to take mathematics examination

		year 10 (4)		year 11 (5)	
GCSE	Higher		(10–12)		(13–15)
	Intermediate		(16–18)		(19–21)
	Foundation		(22–24)		(25–27)

Other examination
(Please specify)

_____ | (28–30) | | (31–33)
_____ | (34–36) | | (37–39)
_____ | (40–42) | | (43–45)

No examination | (46–48) | | (49–51)

2) GCSE Mathematics Examination Results for year 11 (5) summer 1991.

GRADE A (52–54)
GRADE B (55–57)
GRADE C (58–60)
GRADE D (61–63)
GRADE E (64–66)
GRADE F (67–69)
GRADE G (70–72)
U (73–75)

Number not entered or absent (76–78)

Number in the Year Group who left school Easter 1991 (79–80)

Q5. **Absence in previous week**
1) Total number of year 10 (4) and year 11 (5) pupils absent for at least half a day in previous week.

Year 10 (4)   **Year 11 (5)**

Boys   Girls   Boys   Girls

☐ (10–11)   ☐ (12–13)   ☐ (14–15)   ☐ (16–17)

Q6.　1) What subjects are taught in the year 10 (4)? Please tick those where pupils have some element of choice.

	✓		✓
_____	☐	_____	☐
_____	☐	_____	☐ (18)
_____	☐	_____	☐
_____	☐	_____	☐
_____	☐	_____	☐ (19)
_____	☐	_____	☐
_____	☐	_____	☐
_____	☐	_____	☐ (20)
_____	☐	_____	☐
_____	☐	_____	☐

2) What subjects are taught in year 11 (5)? Please tick those where pupils have some element of choice.

	✓		✓
_____	☐	_____	☐
_____	☐	_____	☐ (21)
_____	☐	_____	☐
_____	☐	_____	☐
_____	☐	_____	☐ (22)
_____	☐	_____	☐
_____	☐	_____	☐
_____	☐	_____	☐ (23)

117

Q7. **Extracurricular Activities**

1) List of extracurricular activities. Please include any school community work. Please tick as appropriate if these are available in years 7–9 (1–3), 10–11 (4–5) or both.

Activity	Only yrs 7–9 ✓	Only yrs 10–11 ✓	Yrs 7–11 ✓
_____	☐	☐	☐
_____	☐	☐	☐
_____	☐	☐	☐
_____	☐	☐	☐
_____	☐	☐	☐
_____	☐	☐	☐
_____	☐	☐	☐
_____	☐	☐	☐
_____	☐	☐	☐
_____	☐	☐	☐
_____	☐	☐	☐
_____	☐	☐	☐
	(24) (25)	(26) (27)	(28) (29)

2) Percentage of pupils in years 10 (4) and 11 (5) taking part in extracurricular activities in the last month

Year 10 (4) ☐ % (30–32)

Year 11 (5) ☐ % (33–35)

118

Q8. **Numbers of full-time equivalent staff**

Exclude from teaching staff all instructors, language assistants and peripatetic music teachers. Also exclude all teachers away on secondment; but include any temporary and supply teachers who are filling their posts.

1) Number of full-time staff ☐ (36–38)

2) Number of part-time staff ☐ (39–41)

3) Full-time equivalent of (2) above ☐ (42–44)

Q9. **Teacher-Turnover**

4) Number of full-time staff with less than one year's service in the school ☐ (45–46)

5) Number of part-time staff with less than one year's service in the school ☐ (47–48)

6) Full-time equivalent of (5) above ☐ (49–50)

119

Q10. **Parents**
What means does the school use to involve parents in their children's education?

(10)

(11)

(12)

What information are parents given about school rules?
In particular what are they told about what constitutes justifiable absence?

(13)

(14)

(15)

When do parents have to inform the school if their child is absent?

(16)

(17)

What percentage of parents attend parents' evening? [   ] % (18–20)

Q11. **Homework Policy**
If pupils in any year group are not set the same amount of homework, please explain on what criteria it is set.

(21)

(22)

120

Q12. **Policy on Dress and School Uniform**
1) Policy on school uniform, including sanctions for infringement; policies on PE and games kit etc.

(23)

(24)

(25)

2) If uniform is worn what proportion of children comply.

a) In the school? % (26–28)

(b) In the fourth and fifth years? % (29–31)

3) If there is no school uniform what policy does the school maintain on dress?

(32)

(33)

Q13. Outline the school's system of pastoral care.

(34)

(35)

121

Q14. **Unauthorised Absence**
  1) How do you verify that absence is authorised?

(36)

(37)

  2) What is done in the case of unauthorised absence?
     Please say something about the chain of command in cases of such.

(38)

(39)

(40)

  3) How big a problem do you think unauthorised absence is?

(41)

(42)

(43)

  3b) On a scale of 0–10, where 0 represents no problem at all, and 10 represents
      a problem of extremely serious proportions, please try to give a score to
      indicate the magnitude of the problem of unauthorised absence.

SCORE [   ] (44–45)

  4) Has the situation changed?

(46)

(47)

  5) What do you think causes unauthorised absence? Which pupils are most
     likely to be involved in it? Is ability a related factor?

(48)

(49)

(50)

(51)

Q15. **Post Registration Truancy**
    1) How much Post Registration Truancy do you think there is in year 10 (4)?

                                                                              (52)

                                                                              (53)

    2) How much Post Registration Truancy do you think there is in year 11 (5)?

                                                                              (54)

                                                                                (55)

    3) What is done about Post Registration Truancy, e.g. regular checks?

                                                                              (56)

                                                                                (57)

Q16. Are there any schemes with outside bodies, e.g. compacts with industry, seeking to influence attendance?

                                                                              (58)

                                                                                (59)

Q17. 1) How are good work and behaviour rewarded?

                                                                              (60)

                                                                                (61)

    2) Is good attendance officially recognised in any way?

                                                                              (62)

                                                                                (63)

Q18. What do you think can be done about unauthorised absence from school or Post Registration Truancy?

                                                                              (64)

                                                                                (65)

THANK YOU FOR HELPING US WITH THIS WORTHWHILE STUDY

Printed in the United Kingdom for HMSO
Dd296763 4/94 C15 G3396 10170

Truancy in English Secondary Schools

A Report Prepared for the DFE

9/12

371.
295
TRU

Th